CHARMING

TUSCANY

&

UMBRIA

CHARMING SMALL HOTEL GUIDES
www.charmingsmallhotels.co.uk

TUSCANY & UMBRIA

Including Florence and Siena

EDITED BY

Nicola Swallow

DUNCAN PETERSEN

This new 2006 edition conceived, designed and produced by
Duncan Petersen Publishing Ltd,
C7, Old Imperial Laundry, Warriner Gardens, London SW11 4XW
www.charmingsmallhotels.co.uk

5th Edition

Editorial Director Andrew Duncan
Editor Nicola Swallow
Contributing editor Helen Holubov
Production editor Hermione Edwards
Designer Ian Midson
Photography Gianluca Moggi

This edition published 2006 by
Duncan Petersen Publishing Ltd,
C7, Old Imperial Laundry, Warriner Gardens, London SW11 4XW

Sales representation and distribution in the U.K. and Ireland by
Portfolio Books Limited
Unit 5, Perivale Industrial Park
Horsenden Lane South
Greenford, UB6 7RL
Tel: 0208 997 9000 Fax: 0208 997 9097
E-mail sales@portfoliobooks.com

A CIP catalogue record for this book is available
from the British Library

ISBN 1-903301-44-0

DTP by Duncan Petersen Publishing Ltd
Printed by Polygraf Print, Slovakia

CONTENTS

INTRODUCTION

IN THIS INTRODUCTORY SECTION

Welcome to this new and revised edition of *Charming Small Hotel Guides Tuscany & Umbria*. Recently, we introduced some changes which have made the guide more popular than ever with our readers - see below.

Not only that, but this guide remains unique: the only colour accommodation guide to charming hotels in central Italy.

• *Every hotel has a colour photograph and a full or half page of its own.*

• *The maps have been upgraded.*

• *The layout has been changed in order to take you more quickly to essential information.*

We believe that these are real improvements, rather than change for its own sake. In all other respects, the guide remains true to the values and qualities that make it unique (see opposite), and which have won it so many devoted readers. This is its 6th new edition (including the first edition) since it was first published in 1996. It has sold hundreds of thousands of copies in the U.K., U.S.A. and in five European languages.

WHY ARE WE UNIQUE?

This is the only independently-inspected (no hotel pays for an entry) English-language accommodation guide that:

- has colour photographs for every entry;

- concentrates on places that have real charm and character;

- is highly selective;

- is particularly fussy about size. Most hotels have fewer than 20 bedrooms; if there are more, the hotel must have the feel of a much smaller place. We have found that a genuinely warm welcome is much more likely to be found in a small hotel;

- gives proper emphasis to the description, and doesn't use irritating symbols;

- is produced by a small, non-bureaucratic company with a dedicated team of like-minded inspectors.

See also *'So what exactly do we look for?'*, page 8.

SO WHAT EXACTLY DO WE LOOK FOR? – OUR SELECTION CRITERIA

• A peaceful, attractive setting. Obviously, we make allowances for entries in urban areas.

• A building that is handsome, interesting or historic; or at least with real character.

• Adequate space, but on a human scale. We don't go for places that rely too much on grandeur, or with pretensions that could be intimidating.

• Good taste and imagination in the interior decoration. We reject standardized, chain hotel fixtures, fittings and decorations.

• Bedrooms that look like real bedrooms, not hotel rooms, individually decorated.

• Furnishings and other facilities that are comfortable and well maintained. We like to see interesting antique furniture that is there to be used, not simply revered.

• Proprietors and staff who are dedicated and thoughtful, offering a personal welcome, but who aren't intrusive or overly effusive. *The guest needs to feel like an individual.*

• Interesting food. In Venice, it's increasingly the norm for food to be above average. There are few entries in this guide where the food is not of a high standard.

• A sympathetic atmosphere; an absence of loud people showing off their money; or the 'corporate feel'.

Villa di Piazzano, Tuoro sul Trasimeno

AS SELECTIVE AS EVER
We have maintained the guide's integrity by keeping the selection to around two hundred entries. While there are many apparently charming hotels in this part of the world, we don't believe there to be presently many more than about two hundred really worth writing about. We feel that, if we included more, we would undermine what we're trying to do: produce a guide which is all about places that are more than just a bed for the night. Every time we consider a new hotel, we ask ourselves whether it has that extra special something, regardless of category and facilities, that makes it worth seeking out.

TYPES OF ACCOMMODATION IN THIS GUIDE
Despite its title, the guide does not confine itself to places called hotels or places that behave like hotels. On the contrary, we actively look for places that offer a home-from-home feel (see page 10). We include small- and medium-sized hotels; plenty of traditional Italian guesthouses (*pensioni*) – some offering just bed and breakfast, some offering food at other times of day, too; restaurants with rooms; *agriturismi*, which are usually bed-and-breakfasts on farms or working rural estates; and a useful number of self-catering apartments, in town and country houses, provided they offer something special.

NO FEAR OR FAVOUR
To us, taking a payment for appearing in a guide seems to defeat the object of producing a guide. If money has changed hands, you can't write the whole truth about a hotel, and the selection cannot be nearly so interesting. This self-evident truth seems to us to be proved at least in part by the fact that pay guides are so keen to present the illusion of independence: few admit on the cover that they take payments for an entry, only doing so in small print on the inside.

Not many people realize that on the shelves of bookshops there are many more hotel guides that accept payments for entries than there are independent guides. This guide is one of the few that do not accept any money for an entry.

Villa di Corliano, Rigoli

HOME FROM HOME

Perhaps the most beguiling characteristic of the best places to stay in this guide is the feeling they give of being in a private home – but without the everyday cares and chores of running one. To get this formula right requires a special sort of professionalism: the proprietor has to strike the balance between being relaxed and giving attentive service. Those who experience this 'feel' often turn their backs on all other forms of accommodation – however luxurious.

Tuscany and Umbria for the traveller

It is not difficult to recognize why we chose Tuscany and Umbria as the first regional guide for the series. The region is favoured, par excellence, both with natural and man-made landscapes of incomparable beauty and variety, and its artistic heritage is unequalled in the world. From the Tuscan Coast with its white beaches and pine-shaded coasts to Chianti's rolling hills teeming with cypresses, olives and vines to Umbria, Italy's green heart, visitors will find any form of nature to suit their taste. Travellers through the Garfagnana, in the north-western corner of Tuscany, often think that they have accidentally strayed into some dramatic part of the Alps; while in the still under-explored Maremma, to the south-west, they find cowboys on horse-back tending their herds.

Dotted across the whole region are, of course, many of Italy's most famous *citta d'arte* (art cities), whose names everone knows: Florence, Siena, Volterra, San Gimignano, Perugia, Assisi and Gubbio. But these are only the diamonds in the tiara (and perhaps suffering in recent years from the depredations of mass tourism – they are best seen out of high season unless your idea of a holiday is to stand in long queues for a three-minute ogle of David).

Less well-known gems abound throughout the two regions: Montefalco, known as Umbria's balcony for its remarkable outlook; pretty, medieval Spello, with its ancient history as a Roman settlement; Pienza, a delightful and unique remainder of Renaissance town planning; and the extraordinary town of Pitigliano, dramatically situated on its tufa outcrop.

Much of the delight of travelling this region lies in ignoring the standard tourist trails and just following the road. Do this, and you will always be sure of arriving at some memorable destination which, may well not yet be 'discovered' – by the tourists, or the guide books.

Bedrooms and bathrooms
Most of the hotels in this guide are to be found in old buildings, whether they be farmhouses, medieval castles, Renaissance villas and *palazzi*, former monasteries or just a solid edifice from the 19thC. This guarantees individuality, but it also means that, in the same hotel, the standards of rooms can vary greatly, as, occasionally, do prices. When writing to the hotel, state your requirements - not every monk's cell in a former monastery is blessed with a view. And neither, originally, would it have had a bath room en suite. For the most part, these have been added without undue intrusiveness, but they tend not to be spacious, at least by American standards.

Style varies, but Italians are a meticulously clean people and no bedrooms and bathrooms should be less than acceptable.

Food
Strangely enough, the one place in Italy where a cup of coffee can be disappointing is in a hotel. The pre-prepared beverage lacks the intense flavour of a freshly-made espresso or steaming cappuccino, so if you are fussy about your first cup of the day, ask for one of these. Bed and breakfasts tend to serve 'moka' coffee, made in the characteristic aluminium pot found in all Italian households. In hotels, self-service buffet breakfasts are common, with everything available from cereals to salami, and are ideal for travellers who may not eat properly again until the evening. Most Italians start the day with a cappuccino and a brioche, and in some establishments this may be all you are offered.

Half board is rarely obligatory and often not available, even if the hotel has a restaurant attached, as most visitors like to sample the wide variety of restaurants in an area.

Children
Children are almost always accepted, usually welcomed, in Italian hotels. There are often special facilities, such as cots, high chairs, baby listening and early supper. Check first if they may join parents in the dining room.

HOTELS, VILLAS, LOCANDE, AGRITURISMO
The range of accommodation on offer in Tuscany and Umbria should be enough to satisfy all tastes and most pockets, with a variety of names almost as numerous as those describing types of pasta. 'Hotel' is common enough, but so is its Italian equivalent 'albergo'. 'Villa' can apply either to a town or country hotel and is used by proprietors with some latitude: occasionally one wonders why a nondescript town house or farmhouse should be called a villa while a more elegant building restricts itself to albergo. 'Palazzo' and 'pensione' generally refer to urban accommodation while 'agriturismo' means farmhouse bed-and-breakfast, or indeed, self-catering apartments. 'Residence', 'relais', 'locanda', 'castello' and 'fattoria' are also found.

The variety that one finds under these various names is extraordinary, from world-ranking luxury hotels to relatively simple guesthouses.

TOURIST INFORMATION

Most cities and popular towns have their own tourist offices offering information on local travel, museums, galleries and festivals.

We list below Italy's official public holidays when banks and shops are shut and levels of public transport reduced. In Tuscany and Umbria, like the rest of the country, each town has its own local holiday, usually the feast day of the patron saint, often celebrated with a fair or fireworks.

In addition to these are traditional events peculiar to each locality, such as in Arezzo, where locals joust in full medieval costumes, and in Florence where a lethal version of traditional football is played. The most famous of these is Siena's famous horse-race in Piazza del Campo (the Palio) which takes place in August.

New Year's Day (Capodanno) Jan 1; Epiphany (Epifania) Jan 6; Good Friday (Venerdì Santo); Easter Sunday (Pasqua); Easter Monday (Pasquetta); Liberation Day (Liberazione) April 25; May Day (Festa del Lavoro) May 1; Assumption of the Virgin (Ferragosto) Aug 15; All Saints' Day (Ognissanti) Nov 1; Immaculate Conception (Immacolata Concezione) Dec 8; Christmas Day (Natale) Dec 25; St Stephen's Day (Santo Stefano) Dec 26.

FLIGHTS

The principal airports for Tuscany are at Pisa and Florence, and car hire is available at both. Pisa airport is connected directly to Florence by an hourly train service. Florence airport has a less satisfactory bus connection to the centre. If you are staying in town, try to share a taxi.

Umbria has no major airport of its own, but there is a small one near Perugia.

PET LIKES

These are some of the things that stand out for us in many of the hotels in which we stayed. Maybe they will strike you too.

- Wonderful old buildings, sympathetically restored
- Hotels in superb positions with glorious views
- 'Buffet' breakfasts with fruit, cheese, cold meats and yogurts
- Spotlessly clean bedrooms and bathrooms
- Good quality linen and comfortable pillows

PET HATES

In Florence, too many hotels are happy to coast along rather than strive for perfection. This is for the simple reason that they have a captive audience, a constant influx of tourists who keep occupancy rates at a consistently high level. And prices are very high. Stay outside the city, and you will pay far less for a much larger room. So the hotels which really aim to please, despite their popularity, are the ones which get our highest praise.

- 'Continental' breakfasts with inedible cardboard bread
- Hideous minibars
- Inadequate storage space
- Endless white-tiled bathrooms
- Too many bathrooms with shower only, no bathtub

READERS' REPORTS
To all the hundreds of readers who have written with comments on hotels, a sincere 'thank-you'. We attach great importance to your comments and absorb them into the text each year. Please keep writing.

CHECK THE PRICE FIRST
In this guide we have adopted the system of price bands, rather than giving actual prices as we did in previous editions. This is because prices were often subject to change after we went to press. The price bands refer to the approximate price of a standard double room (high season rates) with breakfast for two people. They are as follows:

€	under 120 Euros
€€	120-180 Euros
€€€	180-260 Euros
€€€€	260-350 Euros
€€€€€	more than 350 Euros

To avoid unpleasant surprises, always check what is included in the price (for example, VAT and service, breakfast, afternoon tea) when making the booking.

HOW TO FIND AN ENTRY
In this guide, the entries are arranged in geographical groups. Tuscany is divided into its provinces: Arezzo, Firenze, Grosseto, Livorno, Lucca, Pisa, Pistoia, Prato and Siena. Umbria is divided into Perugia and Terni. Within each section the entries follow a set sequence:

Entries are arranged alphabetically by city, town or nearest village. If several appear in or near one town, entries are arranged in alpha order by name of hotel.

To find a hotel in a particular area, use the maps following this introduction to locate the appropriate pages.

To locate a specific hotel, whose name you know, or a hotel in a place you know, use the indexes at the back, which list entries both by name and by nearest place name.

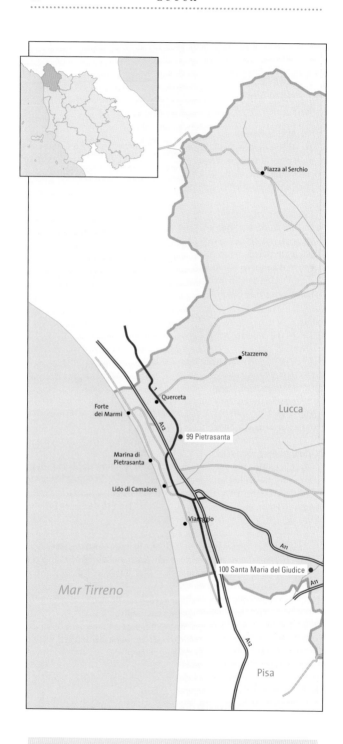

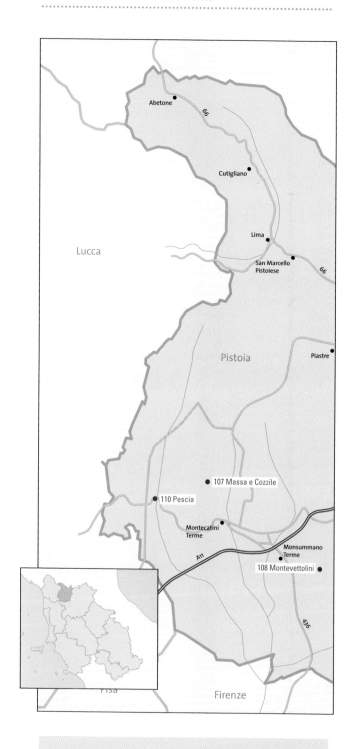

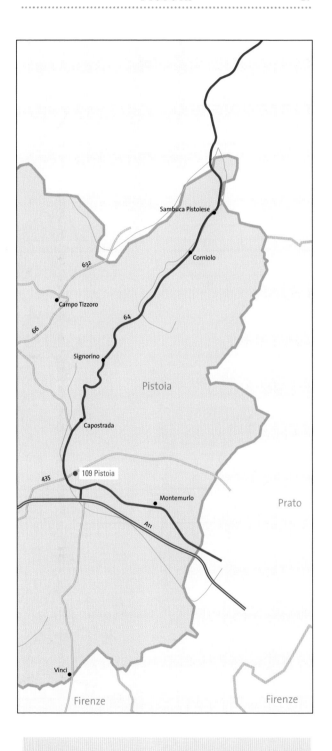

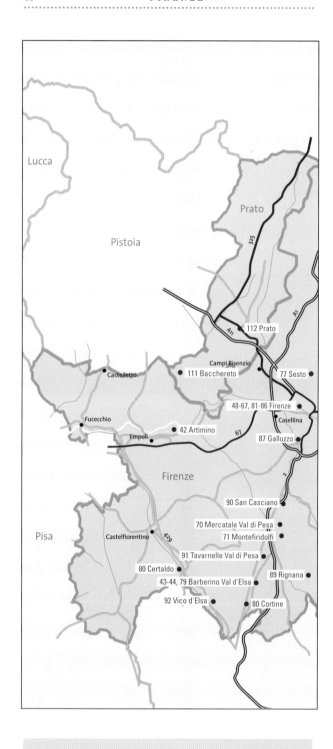

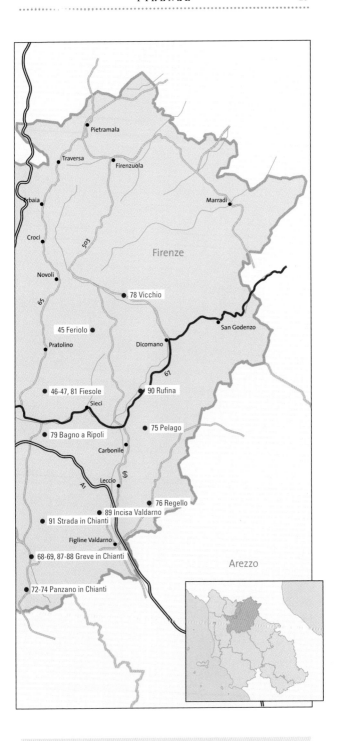

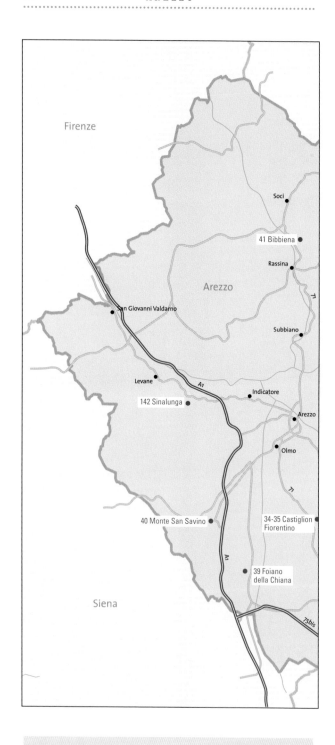

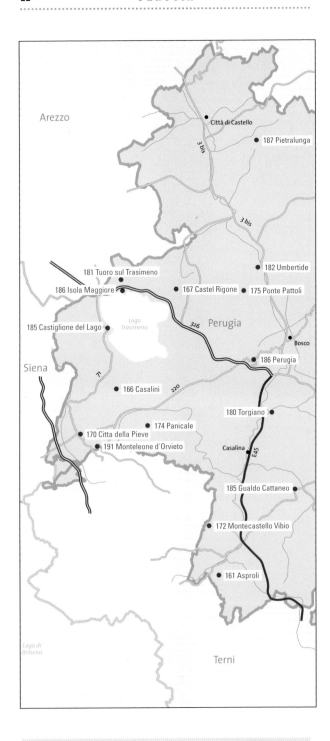

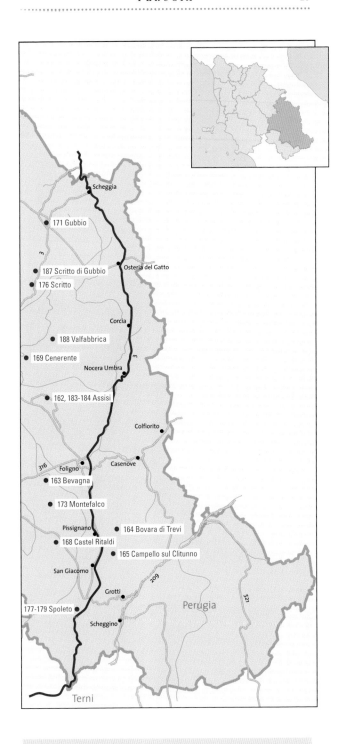

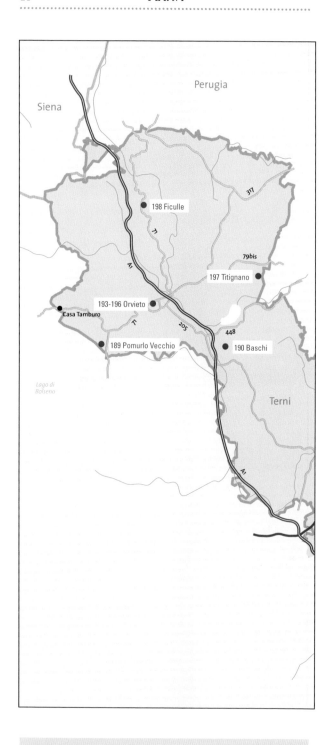

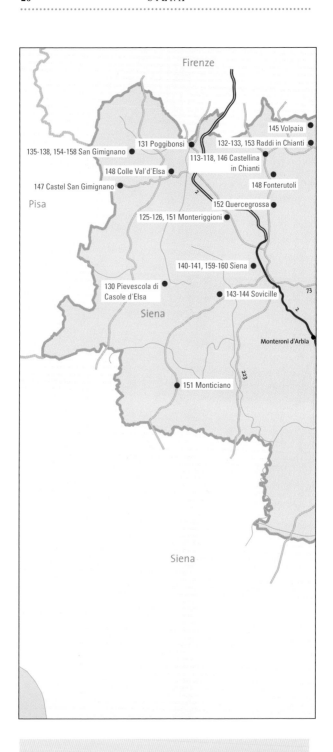

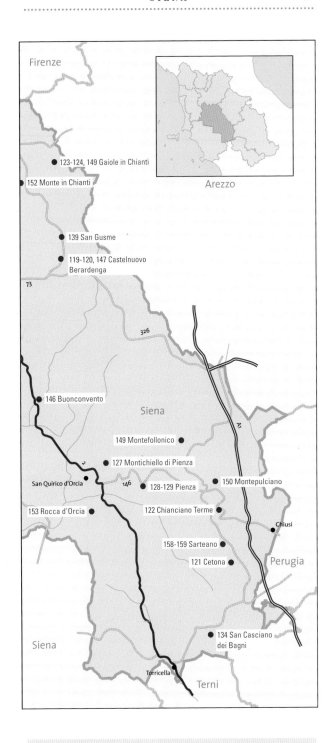

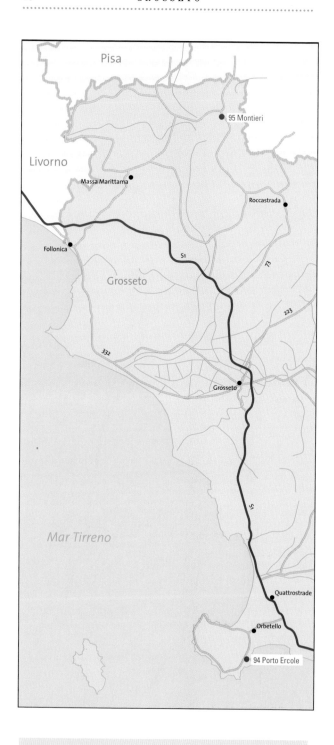

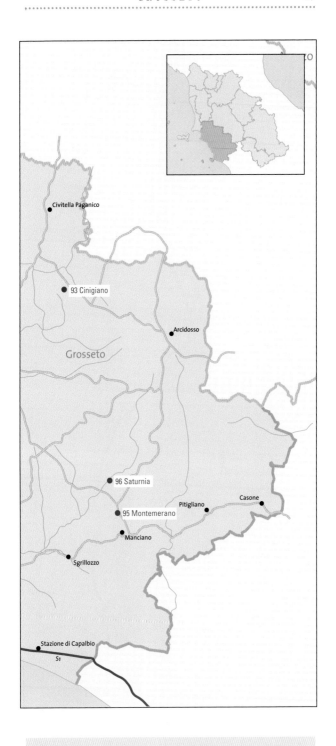

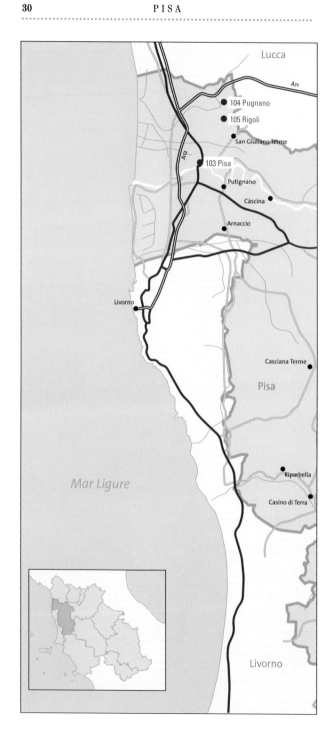

Lucca

A11

● 104 Pugnano
● 105 Rigoli
● San Giuliano Terme

A12

● 103 Pisa
● Putignano
● Càscina
● Arnaccio

Livorno ●

● Casciana Terme

Pisa

● Riparbella

● Casino di Terra

Mar Ligure

Livorno

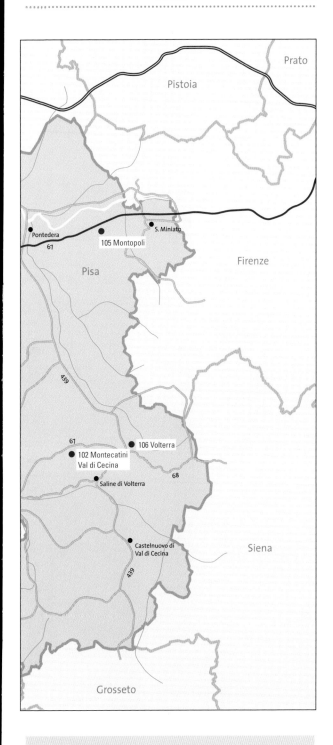

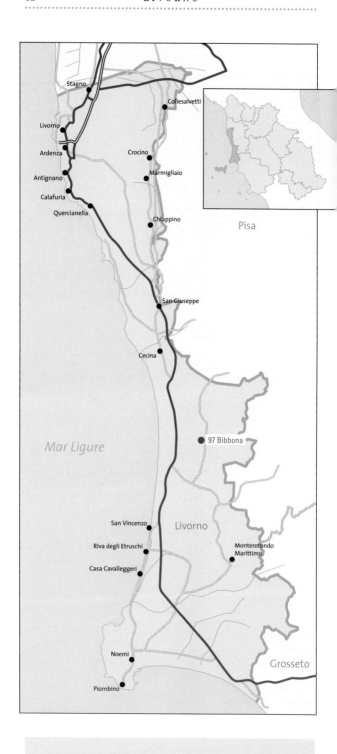

AREZZO

CAPRESE MICHELANGELO

FONTE DELLA GALLETTA
~ MOUNTAIN HOTEL ~

Alpe Faggetta, Caprese Michelangelo, 52033 Arezzo
TEL & FAX (0575) 793925
E-MAIL info@fontedellagalletta.it **WEBSITE** www.fontedellagalletta.it

A WINDING CLIMB through chestnut woods takes you up from the summer heat of the Tiber plain into the walkers' kingdom of the Alpe di Catinaia. At 800 m above sea level, the temperature here rarely reaches 30°C, even on the hottest July day.

The father of the present owners built this stone retreat some 30 years ago in a style that owes more to Switzerland than Tuscany. For most of the year (except weekends and August), it is a tranquil, almost forgotten place. This is its chief charm.

The modern bedrooms in the main building, refurbished in 1994, are small and rather anonymous, while the annexe rooms have been reburbished more recently. The beds are softly sprung, though the proprietor will place a board beneath the mattress if you prefer. Downstairs, the pine-tabled restaurant is anything but cosy. It does, however, offer a tempting range of local dishes according to season.

From the hotel, paths take you up through beech woods to the meadows of the Prate della Regina and the 1,400-m summit of Monte il Castello, with views of the Tiber and east to the Casentino.

~

NEARBY Michelangelo's birthplace at Caprese Michelangelo (6 km).
FOOD breakfast, lunch, dinner
PRICE €
ROOMS 13 double in the hotel & 6 in separate annexe.
FACILITIES restaurant, bar, sitting room, garden, lake
CREDIT CARDS A, MC, V
DISABLED access possible
PETS not accepted
CLOSED 6 Jan-May (except weekends)
LANGUAGES English
PROPRIETORS Berlicchi family

AREZZO

CASTIGLION FIORENTINO

RELAIS SAN PIETRO IN POLVANO
∽ COUNTRY HOTEL ∽

Polvano 3, 52043 Castiglion Fiorentino, Arezzo
TEL (0575) 650100 **FAX** (0575) 650255
E-MAIL polvano@technet.it **WEBSITE** www.polvano.com

SITUATED IN THE HILLS above Castiglion Fiorentino, Polvano is a tiny hamlet comprising a clutch of buildings including this solid stone farmhouse, purchased and restored by the Prottis on retirement, and opened as a small hotel in 1998 which they run with their family.

The house has been renovated with good taste and a modern, clean touch which does not in any way detract from the inherent rustic charateristics of the building (beamed ceilings, bricked archways, terracotta floors and so on). Solid country furniture goes well with sofas upholstered in pale cream fabric, wicker arm chairs and bright, oriental rugs; two comfortble sitting rooms have open fireplaces. The bedrooms, with their wrought iron bed heads and white covers, have a similarly uncluttered feel. In cool weather, food is served in the cosy former stables, but in summer you can eat on the wide, partially covered terrace that runs along one side of the building from which views of the open, unspoiled countryside, are stunning. Antonietta and her daughter-in-law are in charge of the food which, we have heard, is excellent.

This is a delightful place where the emphasis is on peace and tranquility; there are no TV's and children under 12 are discouraged.

∽

NEARBY Cortona (20 km); Arezzo (25 km); Lake Trasimeno (20 km).
LOCATION 10 km east of Castiglion Fiorentino in own grounds; car parking
FOOD breakfast, dinner
PRICE €€€
ROOMS 4 doubles, 1 single, 5 suites, all with bath or shower; all rooms have phone, air conditioning (suites and 2 doubles), hairdrier
FACILITIES sitting rooms, restaurant, breakfast room, terrace, garden, swimming pool **CREDIT CARDS** AE, MC, V
DISABLED no special facilities
PETS not accepted
CLOSED Nov-end Mar
PROPRIETOR Luigi Protti

AREZZO

CASTIGLION FIORENTINO

VILLA SCHIATTI
COUNTRY VILLA

Montecchio, 131 Castiglion Fiorentino, 52043 Arezzo
TEL (0575) 651481 **FAX** (0575) 651482
E-MAIL info@villaschiatti.it **WEBSITE** www.villaschiatti.it

SET AMONG OLIVE GROVES, this substantial Tuscan villa offers the space and simplicity of a family hotel with a number of apartments for longer-term guests. The Schiatti family built their two-towered villa between Castiglion Fiorentino and that most Tuscan of Tuscan hilltowns, Cortona, in the early years of the 19thC, but they lived here for barely a century before their line disappeared.

The present owners, the Bortot family, arrived in 1989 and set about restoring the villa with the minimum of interference to the original structure. Most of its stone and brick floors remain as they were, while the walls are whitewashed and its modest rooms are furnished with unobjectionable reproduction rustic furniture. The interior, however, lacks touches of thoughtful detail.

Signora Patrizia Bortot's quiet and friendly welcome – she speaks fluent English as well as German and French – and the reasonableness of the charges have helped to bring back an increasing number of guests each year. The evening meal, served at eight in the villa's rather impersonal dining-room, is simple and wholesome.

NEARBY Castiglion Fiorenito (3 km); Cortona (8 km).
LOCATION 1 km above the SS71; with gardens and car parking
FOOD breakfast, dinner
PRICE (€)
ROOMS 9 double rooms with shower; three family apartments; all rooms have central heating, TV, phone
FACILITIES sitting room, restaurant, swimming pool, garden
CREDIT CARDS MC,V
DISABLED access difficult **PETS** accepted
CLOSED Jan **LANGUAGES** English, French, German
PROPRIETORS Bortot family

AREZZO

AGRI SALOTTO
~ COUNTRY GUESTHOUSE ~

Burcinella 88, Santa Caterina di Cortona, 52040 Arezzo
TEL (0575) 617417 **FAX** (0575) 638026
E-MAIL info@agrisalotto.it **WEBSITE** www.agrisalotto.it

O N THE PLAIN of Valdichiana, below Cortona clinging to its hillside, can be found a type of farmhouse unique in Tuscany. Constructed during the 18thC when the area was part of the Grand Duchy of Tuscany, they are known as case leopoldiane. On the ground floors were the stables and store-rooms; upstairs were the living quarters and, rising above the main roof, a pigeon-loft. Sadly, many of these have fallen into disrepair over the years, but the Bianchis have made a fine job of restoring one of the few remaining.

On the ground floor is a light and airy, U-shaped space occupied by the restaurant and the sitting area where guests take their aperitivi and coffee on large, comfortable sofas. The essential austerity of the Tuscan rustic style has been softened by antique mirrors and deep blue Chinese vases. Most of the apartments are upstairs, spacious and bright, stylishly furnished with a mixture of old and new pieces. Prices are reasonable and overnight stays are possible (subject to availability in high season). A garden and large swimming pool are at the disposal of guests, and the tranquillity of the surrounding countryside will make you want to prolong your stay.

NEARBY Cortona (10 km); Siena (54 km).
LOCATION in own grounds; ample car parking
FOOD dinner
PRICE €€€
ROOMS 5 apartments (1 two-person, 2 four-person, 2 six-person), all with bath or shower, phone, TV, living room, kitchen
FACILITIES sitting room, restaurant, laundry, garden, swimming pool
CREDIT CARDS not accepted
DISABLED one adapted apartment **PETS** not accepted
CLOSED 3 weeks in Jan
LANGUAGES English, French
PROPRIETORS Silvana and Giovanni Bianchi

AREZZO

CORTONA

IL FALCONIERE
~ COUNTRY VILLA HOTEL ~

San Martino, Cortona, 52044 Arezzo
TEL (0575) 612679 **FAX** (0575) 612927
E-MAIL info@ilfalconiere.com **WEBSITE** www.ilfalconiere.com

T HE PLAIN SURROUNDING Lake Trasimeno, over which Il Falconiere looks, was once the scene of some of Hannibal's fiercest battles against the Romans. Nowadays the only carnage takes place on the A1 *autostrada,* but Il Falconiere is such a haven of civilized living that you will never realize that you are only twenty minutes away from one of Italy's riskiest tourist experiences.

Located just outside Cortona, the main villa (built in the 17thC around an earlier fortified tower) is set in landscaped grounds of olives, rosemary hedges, fruit trees and roses, and the old lemon house is now a Michelin starred restaurant. Meticulous attention has been given to every aspect of decoration and furnishing, from *trompe-l'oeil* number scrolls outside each room to hand-embroidered window hangings and finest bed linen. Persian rugs and handsome antiques rest easily on uneven, original terracotta floors. In the pigeon loft of the old tower, reached by a narrow, stone spiral staircase, is a small bedroom with an unsurpassed view of the Valdichiana.

A villa nearby has recently been converted to create eight new bedrooms with their own breakfast room and pool. The estate produces its own excellent wine and olive oil, and cooking courses are organised too. A recent report praises the hotel unequivocally: 'Everything combines to make this one of the most stylish hotels in Italy.'

NEARBY Cortona (3 km); Arezzo (29 km); Lake Trasimeno (10 km).
LOCATION just outside Cortona overlooking Valdichiana; car parking
FOOD breakfast, lunch, dinner
PRICE €€€€
ROOMS 13 double, 6 suites; all with bath or shower; all rooms have phone, TV, air conditioning, minibar, hairdrier, safe
FACILITIES swimming pools (May-Sep), gardens, restaurant
CREDIT CARDS AE, DC, V **DISABLED** no special facilities
PETS yes but not in rooms **CLOSED** earlyJan-mid Feb
LANGUAGES English, French, German **PROPRIETORS** Riccardo Baracchi and Silvia Regi

AREZZO

CORTONA

SAN MICHELE
TOWN HOTEL

Via Guelfa 15, Cortona, 52044 Arezzo
TEL (0575) 604348 **FAX** (0575) 630147
E-MAIL info@hotelsanmichele.net **WEBSITE** www.hotelsanmichele.net

IT MIGHT SOUND like an easy matter to turn a fine Renaissance palace into a hotel of character, but we have seen too many examples of good buildings brutalised by excessive and unwanted luxury, over-modernization and an almost wilful blindness to the original style, to not be delighted when the job has been properly done.

The Hotel San Michele has steered a precise course between the twin dangers of unwarranted adventurousness and lame timidity. White plaster and stark beams are complemented with rich modern fabrics, and sofas of the finest leather are strewn about terracotta floors that seem glazed with a rich wax. Carefully-placed lights emphasize the gracefully interlocking curves of the cortile. The common rooms are full of such stylish features as frescoed friezes and immense carved stone fireplaces.

The bedrooms are more modest in style, with wrought iron beds and rustic antiques; one recent report states that they are in need of refurbishment while another says hers was decidedly cramped. Some of the more spacious ones have an extra mezzanine to provide separate sleeping and sitting areas. One guest felt that the welcome was somewhat impersonal and that there was a 'faint shadow of the corporate feel' to this hotel.

NEARBY Arezzo (29 km); Perugia (51 km); Diocesan Museum.
LOCATION in middle of town; garage nearby
FOOD breakfast only
PRICE €€€
ROOMS 40 double and twin, and 3 suites; all with bath or shower; all rooms have phone, TV, minibar, air conditioning, hairdrier
FACILITIES sitting room, breakfast room, conference room
CREDIT CARDS AE, DC, MC, V
DISABLED access possible
PETS small dogs accepted **CLOSED** 15 Jan-6 Mar
LANGUAGES English, French, German **PROPRIETOR** Paopo Alunno

AREZZO

FOIANO DELLA CHIANA

VILLA FONTELUNGA
∼ COUNTRY VILLA ∼

Via Cunicchio 5, Foiano della Chiana, 52045 Arezzo
TEL (0575) 660410 **FAX** (0575) 661963
E-MAIL sales@tuscanholiday.com **WEBSITE** www.villafontelunga.com

WHEN THREE FRIENDS decided to open a hotel across the Valdichiana from Cortona, they wanted to avoid the archetypal Tuscan style in favour of something a little different. Villa Fontelunga is the result.

The elegant 19thC patrician villa has sweeping views. A wide gravel terrace in front of the house gives way to sloping lawns and olive trees, while an ingenious outdoor living room complete with fireplace and hints of Morocco provides a lounging spot for hot, lazy afternoons or balmy evenings. Inside, the eclectic, unfussy contemporary design feels both stylish and lived-in. The hub of the house is the open-plan kitchen, eating and sitting area complete with crackling open fire, sofas and coffee tables piled with glossy magazines. The airy bedrooms are simply furnished with a mix of antiques and design pieces. Bathrooms are no-frills white. There is also a romantic little cottage suite in the grounds and three self-catering houses nearby.

The villa is run along sociable, house party lines, and 'Dinner Parties' are held twice a week when everybody eats together. This hip, casual yet classy retreat will appeal to a young crowd and makes a great base for exploring the area's many artistic treasures...if you can drag yourself away.

∼

NEARBY Cortona (20 km); Arezzo (28 km); Montepulciano (20 km).
LOCATION On hillside off the SS 327 about 4 km north of Foiano della Chiana; ample car parking
FOOD breakfast, light lunch on request, dinner on Tues and Fri, light dinner on Mon, Thurs & Sun
PRICE €€€€
ROOMS 8 doubles and 1 twin, all with bath or shower; all rooms have air conditioning, hairdrier, CD player, one with TV/DVD. 3 self catering houses sleeping from 2-6 **FACILITIES** dining room, sitting room, terraces, garden, pool, tennis courts, bikes **CREDIT CARDS** AE, DC, MC, V **DISABLED** one ground floor room
PETS small dogs **CLOSED** end Oct-week before Easter **PROPRIETORS** Paolo Kastelec, Simon Carey, Philip Robinson

AREZZO

MONTE SAN SAVINO

CASTELLO DI GARGONZA
~ HILLTOP CASTLE ~

Gargonza, Monte San Savino, 52048 Arezzo
TEL (0575) 847021/22/23 **FAX** (0575) 847054
E-MAIL gargonza@gargonza.it **WEBSITE** www.gargonza.it

A TREE-LINED ROAD sweeps up the hill alongside the castle walls and brings you into the main square of this fortress-village, dominated by a stately crenellated tower where in more dangerous days lookouts surveyed the Valdichiana below for signs of approaching enemies. The village is as it was centuries ago, a jumble of stone houses connected by crooked paths. Traffic is not allowed in the castle area (except for loading and unloading baggage) and there is a hushed silent atmosphere which at night seems almost eerie – but don't let that put you off.

The *foresteria,* or guesthouse, has seven fairly Spartan rooms rentable for a minimum of three days in high season. Twenty five self-catering apartments (named after past occupants) are let on a weekly basis and offer good value for groups of families. They are comfortable and mostly spacious with new bathrooms, pretty co-ordinating fabrics, working fireplaces and cleverly concealed kitchen units. Note that housekeeping is only available on request.

Breakfast is served in the *frantoio* (the old olive press), which also houses a sitting room graced with the only TV on the premises. Just below the walls, a rustic restaurant serves excellent local specialities including homemade pici with duck sauce and superb Chainina beef. The addition of a large pool, on a terrace bordered by rosemary hedges, is very welcome.

~

NEARBY Siena (35 km); Arezzo (25 km).
LOCATION 8 km W of Monte San Savino, off the SS 73; car parking outside walls
FOOD breakfast, lunch, dinner
PRICE €€
ROOMS 10 double in main guesthouse, all with bath or shower; 25 self-catering houses; all rooms have phone, hairdrier; main guesthouse rooms have minibar
FACILITIES 4 sitting rooms (2 for meetings), bar, restaurant, swimming pool, bowls
CREDIT CARDS AE, DC, MC, V **DISABLED** not suitable **PETS** not accepted
CLOSED 3 weeks Nov **LANGUAGES** English, French, German
PROPRIETOR Conte Roberto Guicciardini

AREZZO

BORGO ANTICO
TOWN HOTEL

Via Bernardo Dovizi 18,
Bibbiena, 52011 Arezzo

TEL (0575) 536445/46
FAX (0575) 536447
E-MAIL none
FOOD breakfast, lunch, dinner
PRICE €
CLOSED never

A USEFUL ADDRESS in a part of Tuscany not over-supplied with recommendable hotels in spite of the great countryside. Bedrooms are comfortable and modern, lacking in character but serviceable and fairly spacious. The public areas retain more of the character of the original palazzo, although it has to be said that they may not be decorated to your taste. There is a bar and a restaurant, rather oddly called La Locanda Web, because of the presence of an internet point, which may have seemed a grand feature at the time, but seems a little odd now. Golf, swimming, tennis, riding and a national park nearby.

CORYS
COUNTRY HOTEL

Torreone, 7 Cortona, Arezzo

TEL (0575) 605141
FAX (0575) 631443
E-MAIL info@corys.it
WEBSITE www.corys.it
FOOD breakfast, lunch, dinner
PRICE €€
CLOSED never

A USEFUL STOPOVER ADDRESS clinging to the hill just outside Cortona, whose charm is mainly in a stupendous view down the Valdichiana to Lake Trasimeno. In the pleasant dining room, with attractive lighting, owners Silvia and Renato offer tasting menus of mushrooms, truffles and seafood, and a large selection of wines, especially Tuscan ones. It's also possible to dine on the terrace so as to take in the view (although this is not open to non-residents). In the restored building everything is spotless, and though rooms are standardised (with fridge as well as satellite TV and phone) and without much character. A reader speaks of a friendly small-hotel atmosphere and helpful staff, though another does mention a dull breakfast and 'overcooked' food at dinner.

FIRENZE

ARTIMINO

PAGGERIA MEDICEA
~ COUNTRY HOTEL ~

Viale Papa Giovanni XXIII, Artimino, 59015 Firenze
TEL (055) 8718081 **FAX** (055) 8751470
E-MAIL artimino@tin.it **WEBSITE** www.artimino.com

VILLA ARTIMINO, a Medici villa built when the family was at the height of its powers, stands high in the hills of the wine producing district of Carmignano, west of Florence. Money from their banking activities and a sense of style that made them the greatest ever patrons of the arts combined to make this one of their most magnificent country residences. The villa is a museum, but the former stables are now this excellent hotel.

They certainly did their grooms well. Both sides of the long, low building are flanked by beautifully articulated loggias on to which most of the bedrooms open. The rooms themselves are spacious and shadily cool in summer; in other seasons visitors may find that the loggia prevents enough light from getting in. Each has a large stone fireplace so that the roof, like the villa's beside, is cluttered with chimneys standing to attention like toy soldiers.

Downstairs, the stalls have been turned into breakfast rooms and sitting areas full of comfortable couches, interesting books, old rugs and prints. The gardens look on to the city simmering on the sultry plain below and, even in July, catch a cool evening breeze.

~

NEARBY Prato (15 km); Florence (24 km); Etruscan museum.
LOCATION 24 km NW of Florence; car parking
FOOD breakfast, lunch, dinner
PRICE €€
ROOMS 36 double and twin with bath or shower, 1 single with shower; all have central heating, air conditioning, minibar, TV, phone, radio; 44 apartments in village with own pool
FACILITIES breakfast room, sitting room, TV room, restaurant, 2 tennis courts, jogging, swimming pool, mountain bikes, laundry
CREDIT CARDS AE, DC, MC, V
DISABLED ground floor rooms
PETS accepted **CLOSED** 10 days Christmas-New Year **LANGUAGES** English, French
MANAGER Alessandro Gualtieri

FIRENZE

BARBERINO VAL D'ELSA

IL PARETAIO
~ COUNTRY GUESTHOUSE ~

San Filippo, Barberino Val d'Elsa, 50021 Firenze
TEL (055) 8059218 **FAX** (055) 8059231
E-MAIL ilparetaio@tin.it **WEBSITE** www.ilparetaio.it

A GREAT ADDRESS for those interested in horse riding but not to be dismissed by travellers in search of the country life. Strategically located between Florence and Siena, in hilly surroundings, Il Paretaio is a 17thC stone-built farmhouse on its own large estate.

The accommodation is simple but attractive. The ground floor entrance and sitting area was originally a work-room, and still retains the old stone paving. A huge brick arch spans the central space and brick-vaulting contrasts with the plain white walls. Upstairs, the rustic style is continued in the exposed-beam ceilings and worn terracotta floors.

The dining room is particularly attractive with its larch-wood table, ten feet long, where communal meals are served, and a huge open fireplace. Most of the bedrooms are off this room, with country furniture and equestrian prints. The most attractive bedroom is in the dovecot, a mini-tower at the top of the house with pretty little arched windows on three sides looking on to the rolling landscape.

Outside is a riding arena, and a swimming pool.

~

NEARBY Florence (33 km); San Gimignano (21 km); Siena (34 km).
LOCATION 3 km S of Barberino Val d'Elsa
FOOD breakfast, dinner
PRICE €
ROOMS 6 double; two apartments for 4-5 people; reductions for children
FACILITIES garden, swimming pool, horse riding, (all standards and all ages), mountain bikes
CREDIT CARDS not accepted
DISABLED no special facilities
PETS accepted **CLOSED** never
LANGUAGES English, French
PROPRIETORS Giovanni and Cristina de Marchi

FIRENZE

LA CHIARA DI PRUMIANO
~ FARM GUESTHOUSE ~

Strada di Cortine 12, 50021 Barberino Val d'Elsa, Firenze
TEL (055) 8075583 **FAX** (055) 8075678
E-MAIL prumiano@tin.it

WHEN FOUR FAMILIES bought the Chiara di Prumiano (formerly a country residence of the Corsini family) some 15 years ago with plans to make it pay for itself, they took on an enormous project. The estate runs to 40 hectares of land with a grand, albeit rather crumbling, villa at the centre of a small hamlet, complete with its own tiny chapel.

Now run by two of the original owners, the Chiara is a successful business, but the atmosphere is laid-back and alternative. The creeper-clad villa offers modestly furnished but spacious bedrooms, a sitting room of baronial proportions, two dining rooms and various spaces used for seminars and workshops. Other accommodation is in simple, tastefully converted buildings nearby.

Courses are hosted year-round, so the guest may find himself or herself eating at one of the long, communal tables with a Yoga group. The delicious meals are predominantly (but not exclusively) vegetarian and make creative use of home-grown fruit and vegetables, olive oil and wine.

~

NEARBY Siena (40 km); San Gimignano (25 km); Florence (35 km).
LOCATION 4 km SE of Barberino; best approached from the San Donato superstrada
FOOD breakfast; lunch and dinner on request
PRICE €
ROOMS 15 doubles and 2 apartments, 11 with bath or shower
FACILITIES meeting rooms, garden, swimming pool, riding
CREDIT CARDS EC, MC, V
DISABLED access difficult
PETS accepted but please advise when booking
CLOSED Christmas–mid Jan
LANGUAGES English, French, Spanish
PROPRIETORS Gaia Mezzadri and Antonio Pescett

FIRENZE

FERIOLO

CASA PALMIRA
~ COUNTRY GUESTHOUSE ~

Via Faentina, Feriolo, 50030 Polcanto, Firenze
TEL & **FAX** (055) 8409749
E-MAIL info@casapalmira.it **WEBSITE** www.casapalmira.it

LEAVING FLORENCE, THE OLD Faenza road winds through olive groves and cypresses before reaching the beautiful and relatively unknown area of the Mugello, and continuing up and over the Apennines. Casa Palmira is set just off this road in an oasis of green, a converted barn attached to a stone farmhouse with medieval origins.

Stefano and Assunta, the warm and charming hosts, have done a beautiful job on converting the barn into a relaxed and comfortable guesthouse. The ground floor sitting room is spacious and welcoming, with a huge fireplace, squashy sofas and chairs, an open kitchen area where breakfast is prepared, and a dining area. Upstairs, the bedrooms all lead off a lovely sunny landing, and while the public areas have terracotta flagstones, the bedrooms all have beautiful chestnut wood floors made by Stefano (who also made the doors and some of the furniture). Pretty fabrics and patchwork quilts complement warm-coloured walls and dusty green paintwork. There is wonderful walking nearby, mountain bikes to hire, and there is even a hot tub in the garden. Who needs Florence?

~

NEARBY Florence (16 km); Fiesole (9 km).
LOCATION halfway between Florence and Borgo San Lorenzo just off the SS302, Via Faentina (from Florence turn right to Feriolo just past Olmo); car parking
FOOD breakfast, dinner on request
PRICE €
ROOMS 4 double and twin, 1 single, 1 triple, 1 with bath, 6 with shower (although not all are en suite); rooms have hairdrier on request
FACILITIES sitting room, breakfast/dining room, terraces, garden with barbecue, hot tub, swimming pool
CREDIT CARDS not accepted
DISABLED access difficult **PETS** not accepted
CLOSED Jan-Feb
PROPRIETORS Assunta Fiorini and Stefano Mattioli

FIRENZE

FIESOLE

LE CANNELLE
~ TOWN GUESTHOUSE ~

Via Gramsci 52-56, 50014 Fiesole, Firenze
TEL (055) 5978336 **FAX** (055) 5978292
E-MAIL info@lecannelle.com **WEBSITE** www.lecannelle.com

L E CANNELLE'S YOUNG PROPRIETORS, Sara and Simona Corsi, have a father with a building business, so who better to restore these two old town houses on Fiesole's main street, a little way north of the main square? Once finished, he handed over the management of this little bed and breakfast to his two daughters, who have enthusiastically set about their new activity since opening in November 1999.

The cool hills surrounding Fiesole are studded with spectacular villas, and many of the hotels in the area are correspondingly expensive. We are therefore pleased to include Le Cannelle as a low cost, but charming, alternative. It has been carefully decorated in simple, yet comfortable style. Bedrooms are quite spacious, and one even has a duplex with two single beds at the top. Two rooms offer lovely views of the hills to the north. Those on the somewhat noisy street have double glazing. The blue and white bathrooms are spotless. The pretty room where Sara and Simona prepare breakfast is, unfortunately, right on the street.

~

NEARBY Florence (8 km); Roman amphitheatre.
LOCATION on main street N of main square; car parking
FOOD breakfast
PRICE €€
ROOMS 1 single, 2 double, 1 triple, 1 family, all with bath or shower; all rooms have phone, TV, air conditioning
FACILITIES breakfast room
CREDIT CARDS AE, DC, MC, V
DISABLED not suitable
CLOSED Jan-Feb
LANGUAGES English, French
PROPRIETORS Sara and Simona Corsi

FIRENZE

VILLA SAN MICHELE
∾ CONVERTED MONASTERY ∾

Via di Doccia 4, Fiesole, 50014 Firenze
TEL (055) 59451 **FAX** (055) 598734 **E-MAIL** reservations@villasanmichele.net
WEBSITE www.orient/expresshotels.com

A HOTEL SO EXPENSIVE that even its cheapest single rooms, which are rather small, lie well outside the price range represented by our symbols: one of the better suites will cost you nearly three million lire, enough to pay dinner for at least ten people at Florence's finest restaurant. At these prices one expects transcendent perfection, but we have the feeling that part of the frisson of staying at San Michele is having paid so much in the first place.

Cost aside, the hotel is undoubtedly among the finest in the guide, both for its location, and for the character of its buildings, whose post-war restoration has been successful in removing some insensitive 19thC embellishments and repairing bomb damage. The dignified façade with its porticoed loggia is based on a design attributed to Michaelangelo, and once you pass through the doors you have the odd sensation of checking in to a former church. Antiques, acquired without heed of expense, abound, although there is also some modern furniture. Bedrooms in the new annex have less character than those in the original building. The chic restaurant serves meals on a lovely, covered lemon terrace.

NEARBY Florence (6 km); Fiesole (1 km); Roman theatre, cathedral, monastery of San Francesco.
LOCATION just below Fiesole on Florence-Fiesole road; car parking
FOOD breakfast, lunch, dinner
PRICE €€€€€
ROOMS 25 double and twin, 15 suites, all with bath and shower; all rooms have phone, air conditioning TV, heating
FACILITIES sitting rooms, bar, restaurant, terrace, swimming pool, private city bus shuttle
CREDIT CARDS AE, DC, MC, V
DISABLED one suitable room **PETS** small dogs only (not in restaurant or near pool)
CLOSED end Nov-mid Mar **LANGUAGES** English, French, German, Spanish
MANAGER Maurizio Saccani

FIRENZE

FLORENCE

ANNALENA
～ TOWN GUESTHOUSE ～

Via Romana 34, 50125 Firenze
TEL (055) 222402 **FAX** (055) 222403
E-MAIL annalena@hotelannalena.it **WEBSITE** www.annalena.it

ONE OF FLORENCE'S traditional *pensioni*, and, in spite of new owners, still very much in the old style, the Annalena is located opposite the back entrance to the beautiful Boboli gardens. Many of the bedrooms look out on to a horticultural centre next door, the best give on to a long veranda. Luckily, none of them has windows on the busy Via Romana.

The 14th century *palazzo* has an intriguing past involving, in its early days, the tragic Annalena (a young noblewoman) and, during the war, foreign refugees fleeing from Mussolini's police. Today, while no luxury hotel, the Annalena offers solid comforts not without a hint of style, and at resonable prices. The huge public room (serving as reception, bar, sitting and breakfast rooms) is a bit dreary, but the bedrooms are lovely: spacious and full of light from tall windows which take full advantage of views of the garden below and the picturesque backs of neighbouring houses. Smart new fabrics and a lick of paint have done wonders for rooms that had been allowed to get a little shabby.

Guests lucky enough to have a room with a terrace should order breakfast there: so much nicer than a rather cramped table in the airless 'salon'.

～

NEARBY Pitti Palace; Boboli Gardens; Ponte Vecchio; Santo Spiritoi.
LOCATION south of the river, 3 minutes' walk S of the Pitti Palace; public car parking nearby
FOOD breakfast
PRICE €€
ROOMS 16 double and twin, 4 single, all with bath or shower; all rooms have phone, TV, air conditioing, minibar, safe, hairdrier
FACILITIES sitting room/bar/breakfast room
CREDIT CARDS AE, DC, MC, V
DISABLED no special facilities
PETS accepted
CLOSED never
PROPRIETOR Icilio Marazzini

FIRENZE

FLORENCE

ANTICA DIMORA
~ TOWN GUESTHOUSE ~

Via San Gallo 72, 50129 Firenze
TEL (055) 4627296 **FAX** (055) 4635450
E-MAIL info@anticadimorafirenze.it **WEBSITE** www.anticadimorafirenze.it

LEA GULMANELLI AND JOHANAN Vitta's by now well established 'mini-chain' of elegant yet reasonably priced guesthouses has enjoyed huge success in Florence since they opened their first place in 1994. The Antica Dimora is the newest and most up-market of the five, and is situated just north of the Duomo. The entrance to the elegant, second floor apartment is through an anonymous doorway and rather austere entrance hall, but, once inside, the atmosphere is warm and welcoming. Classical music plays softly in the background and a table is laid for guests to help themselves to coffee, tea or *vin santo* in the brightly lit breakfast/sitting room. The six carefully furnished bedrooms are painted in pastel hues with pretty bathrooms to match. Beds have smart striped bedheads, and four-posters (of which there are several) are hung with linen or shot silk which matches the curtains. Bright oriental rugs sit on cotto floors, and botanical prints adorn the walls. Rooms at the back of the building are quieter: one has a private, flower-filled terrace. If there's no room at the Antica Dimora, you can always stay at the slightly cheaper (but no less charming) Residenza Johlea up the road, under the same management.

~

NEARBY Duomo; Museo di San Marco; San Lorenzo & Central Market.
LOCATION on street north of Duomo; paid car parking nearby
FOOD breakfast
PRICE €€
ROOMS 6 doubles and twins, all with bath or shower; all rooms have phone, DVD, TV, safe, air conditioning, hairdrier, minibar
FACILITIES breakfast/sitting room, lift
CREDIT CARDS not accepted
DISABLED no special faciliies
PETS small, on request **CLOSED** never
PROPRIETORS Lea Gulmanelli and Johanan Vitta

FIRENZE

FLORENCE

CLASSIC
~ TOWN HOTEL ~

Viale Machiavelli 25, 50125 Firenze
Tel (055) 229351 **Fax** (055) 229353
E-MAIL ferme.du.vert@wanadoo.fr **WEBSITE** www.fermeduvert.com

STANDING IN ITS OWN LUSH GARDEN and rubbing shoulders with some of the most impressive residences in Florence, this pink-washed villa is on a leafy avenue just five minutes from Porta Romana, the old gate into the south of the city. A private residence until 1991, the house was rescued from decay and turned into a comfortable and friendly hotel which maintains admirably reasonable prices.

Bedrooms vary in size, but all are fairly spacious with parquet floors, original plasterwork, antique furniture and pretty bedspreads. Two have frescoes, and another hosts an impressive fireplace. The high ceilings on the first floor allow for a duplex arrangement with extra space for beds or sitting areas on a higher level, while top floor rooms have sloping, beamed attic ceilings and air conditioning. A romantic annexe suite tucked away in the garden, complete with tiny kitchen area, offers extra privacy for the same price as a standard double.

In warmer weather, breakfast is served outside under a pergola, but even in winter the conservatory allows for a sunny - possibly even a warm - start to the day.

~

NEARBY Pitti Palace, Piazzale Michelangelo, Museo La Specola.
LOCATION In residential area five minutes' walk from Porta Romana; car parking
FOOD breakfast
PRICE €€
ROOMS 2 single, 17 double and twin, 1 suite, all with bath or shower; all rooms have phone, TV; air conditioning, safe, hairdrier
FACILITIES breakfast room, garden, conservatory
CREDIT CARDS AE, DC, MC, V
DISABLED lift; ground floor bedrooms
PETS accepted **CLOSED** 2 weeks in Aug
LANGUAGES English, French, German
PROPRIETOR Corinne Kraft

FIRENZE

FLORENCE

GALLERY HOTEL ART
~ TOWN HOTEL ~

Vicolo del' Oro 5, 50120 Florence
TEL (055) 27263 **FAX** (055) 268557
E MAIL gallery@lungarnohotels.com **WEBSITE** www.fermeduvert.com

IT WAS NO PROBLEM to stretch our normal size limit to include Florence's newest hotel: first because it is unique, and second because it feels like a much smaller place. In a quiet piazzetta just a few steps from the Ponte Vecchio, the Gallery is a temple of contemporary design, a combination of east and west which provides endless curiosities to look at and to touch. While the style is minimalist, it avoids being cold. Colours are muted and restful. Greys, creams, taupes and white dominate, while dark African wood is used throughout to add warmth and contrast. Contemporary art hangs on the walls, and throughout the public rooms there is an impressive feeling of space.

A smart bar with squashy sofas houses a large video screen, while the reading room is dominated by a huge bookcase filled with interesting volumes to be browsed through at leisure. Inviting knee rugs are draped over the pale sofas, almost begging the guest to relax with a book.

Bedrooms vary in size, but are all along the same stylish, sober lines. The bathrooms, with classic chrome fittings, are splendid.

~

NEARBY Ponte Vecchio, Pitti Palace, Uffizi.
LOCATION in centre of town next to Ponte Vecchio with valet car parking nearby
FOOD breakfast, lunch, dinner
PRICE ©©©©
ROOMS 65 rooms, 9 suites and junior suites, all with bath or shower, phone, TV, air conditioning, hairdrier, safe
FACILITIES library, bar, breakfast room, terrace
CREDIT CARDS AE, DC, MC, V
DISABLED 2 adapted rooms
PETS small dogs accepted
CLOSED never
LANGUAGES English, French, German, Spanish, Japanese
MANAGER Alessio Ianna

FIRENZE

FLORENCE

HELVETIA & BRISTOL
～ TOWN HOTEL ～

Via dei Pescioni 2, 50123 Firenze
TEL (055) 26651 **FAX** (055) 288353 **E MAIL** information.hbf@royaldemeure.com
WEBSITE www.hotelhelvetiabristolfirenze.it

T HE HELVETIA was originally a Swiss-owned hotel right in the centre of
Florence which added the name Bristol to attract 19thC British travellers. Illustrious past guests include Stravinsky, Bertrand Russell and
Gabriel d'Annunzio. After 1945, it gradually fell into decay until new management took it over and began restoration in 1987, sparing no expense in
their imaginative recreation of a 19thC luxury hotel.

Those with classical tastes, used to the stark simplicity of the Tuscan
style, may find the results cloying and indigestible, but others will enjoy
the rich colour schemes and heavy, dark antiques. The least overwhelming
room is a 1920s winter garden where breakfast is served; it is full of handsome cane furniture and potted palms, with a green-tinted glass ceiling.
The bedrooms are, if anything, even more ornate than the public rooms.
Antiques, Venetian mirrors and chandeliers plus swathes of rich fabric
add to the opulence. One of the finest features of the hotel is its extensive
collection of prints and pictures. Staff and service are smooth and professional. In 2000 the hotel extended into the next door building, adding
18 new doubles and three suites. The restaurant has also had a complete
overhaul, and is now done out in vibrant oranges and reds - the result is
less formal than before.

～

NEARBY Ponte Vecchio, Uffizi, Palazzo Vecchio, Palazzo Pitti.
LOCATION in centre of town, opposite Palazzo Strozzi, W of Piazza Repubblica;
public car parking nearby
FOOD breakfast, lunch, dinner
PRICE €€€€€
ROOMS 67 double and twin, singles and suites, all with bath or shower; all rooms
have phone, TV, CD player, hairdrier, minibar, air conditioning
FACILITIES sitting rooms, restaurant, bar, winter garden
CREDIT CARDS AE, DC, MC, V **DISABLED** some facilities
PETS not accepted **CLOSED** never **LANGUAGES** English, French, German, Spanish
MANAGER Pietro Panelli

FIRENZE

FLORENCE

HERMITAGE
~ TOWN GUESTHOUSE ~

Vicolo Marzio 1, Piazza del Pesce, 50122 Firenze
TEL (055) 287216 **FAX** (055) 212208
E-MAIL florence@hermitagehotel.com **WEBSITE** www.hermitagehotel.com

A HOTEL YOU ARE HARDLY LIKELY to stumble across, despite its central location next to the Ponte Vecchio on the north side of the Arno. A discreetly placed entrance in a small alleyway, opposite the porticos supporting Vasari's corridor, admits you to a lift taking you up five floors to the
reception and its friendly, international staff.

The Hermitage is like a cappuccino: the best bits are on top and matters
become more mundane as you descend. The roof terrace, filled with flowers in terracotta pots and shade provided by a pergola, commands unrivalled views of the city. Sitting there at breakfast, you can plan the day's
excursions almost without the aid of a map. The sitting room (and bar)
looks directly on to the Ponte Vecchio and the Oltrarno.

The Hermitage was once no more than one of the typical, older style
pension that are becoming rare in Florence. But it has had a marked
facelift and is now more tasteful, well kept (and expensive) than average.
It also has touches of luxury: all rooms have Jacuzzis or showers. After the
Uffizi bombing in 1993, the streets around were banned to traffic, so noise
is not a problem – assisted by the judicious, although not always sufficient,
double glazing on the busier riverside aspect.

~

NEARBY Ponte Vecchio, Uffizi, Palazzo Vecchio, Palazzo Pitti, Duomo.
LOCATION right beside the Ponte Vecchio; private pay car parking nearby
FOOD breakfast, snacks
PRICE €€€
ROOMS 28 double and twin, 24 with bath, 4 with shower; all rooms have phone,
central heating, air conditioning, hairdrier, safe, satellite TV
FACILITIES sitting room, bar, breakfast room, roof terrace
CREDIT CARDS V, MC,
DISABLED access difficult **PETS** small dogs accepted **CLOSED** never
LANGUAGES English, German, Portuguese
PROPRIETOR Vincenzo Scarcelli

FIRENZE

FLORENCE

J AND J
～ TOWN HOTEL ～

Via di Mezzo 20, 50121 Firenze
TEL (055) 2345005 **FAX** (055) 240282
E-MAIL jandj@dada.it **WEBSITE** www.hoteljandj.com

THIS HIGHLY INDIVIDUAL hotel in a former convent of the 16thC is to be found, off the usual tourist routes, in a residential part of the old city centre. However, it is still convenient for visiting all the obligatory Florentine museums, with the advantage of peace and quiet when you get back to the hotel in the evening.

Perhaps it was the owner's training as an architect that gave him the confidence to combine old and new so strikingly in the decoration and furnishings. The building is, in fact, two, separated by a terracotta-paved cloister where breakfast is served during the summer months. In front of this is a lovely light room with painted wicker furniture and a decorated vaulted ceiling, separated from the cloister only by the glassed-in arches. The sitting room next door combines original features with pale modern furniture and mellow lighting.

Some of the bedrooms are enormous, possibly because they used to be studio flats, and could sleep a family of four in comfort. Each one is different in style, furnished with antiques and hand-woven fabrics. A word of warning - the stairs are very steep and there is no lift.

～

NEARBY Santa Croce, San Marco, Santissima Annunziata.
LOCATION a few minutes' walk E of the Duomo
FOOD breakfast
PRICE €€€€
ROOMS 12 double and twin, 7 suites, all with bath; all rooms have phone, TV, minibar, air conditioning, hairdrier
FACILITIES sitting room, breakfast room, courtyard, bar
CREDIT CARDS AE, DC, MC, V
DISABLED no special facilities
PETS not accepted **CLOSED** never
LANGUAGES English, French, German
PROPRIETOR James Cavagnari

FIRENZE

FLORENCE

J.K. PLACE
~ TOWN HOTEL ~

Piazza Santa Maria Novella 7, 50123 Firenze
TEL (055) 2645181 **FAX** (055) 2658387
E-MAIL jkplace@jkplace.com **WEBSITE** www.jkplace.com

OCCUPYING A TALL, elegant town house on Piazza Santa Maria Novella, and opened in May 2003, J.K. Place is Florence's newest and most captivating boutique hotel. To the right is Alberti's glorious symmetrical church façade; you can almost ignore the shabbiness of the square itself. Once inside the discreet entrance, the cares of the world and the dust of the city really do seem to fade into the restful cream and grey colour scheme, the soft music, the heady scent of flowers, the flickering candle light and the bend-over-backwards-to-help attention of the charming staff. While not for those on a lean budget, and much beloved by the fashion crowd, this hotel is not at all stuffy or intimidating.

The decoration is a seductive contemporary take on neo-classical style. Rooms are filled with comfortable furniture, interesting art and covetable *objets*. A fire burns in the cosy sitting room where arm chairs and sofas are draped with cashmere throws. Breakfast is served at a big polished antique table in the glassed-in courtyard or in your room. Bedrooms continue along the same stylish lines (although some are very small) while bathrooms are naturally magnificent. Views from the rooftop terrace take in the whole city.

~

NEARBY Santa Maria Novella; Ponte Vecchio; Uffizi; Palazzo Vecchio.
LOCATION in the centre of town with lift; private garage nearby
FOOD breakfast, snacks
PRICE €€€€€
ROOMS 13 double and twin, 7 suites, all with bath or shower; all rooms have phone, TV, DVD, CD, air conditioning, minibar, safe, hairdrier
FACILITIES sitting rooms, breakfast room, bar, roof terrace
CREDIT CARDS AE, DC, MC, V
DISABLED adapted rooms
PETS accepted if small
CLOSED never
GENERAL MANAGER Omri Kafri

FIRENZE

FLORENCE

LOGGIATO DEI SERVITI
∾ TOWN HOTEL ∾

Piazza SS. Annunziata 3, 50122 Firenze
TEL (055) 289 592 **FAX** (055) 289595
E-MAIL info@loggiatodeiservitihotel.it **WEBSITE** www.loggiatodeiservitihotel.it

SITUATED IN A MOST ADMIRABLE location in the Piazza SS Annunziata, the Loggiato dei Serviti is opposite Brunelleschi's Ospedale degli Innocenti, and underneath a portico decorated with ceramic medallions by della Robbia. Florence's most beautiful square, however, is popular with tramps and vagabonds who sleep under the loggia there (even in December). The combination of their noise and the church bells at night might well disturb a light sleeper.

The interior is cool and restrained: rooms are individually decorated, furnished with antiques and well-chosen modern pieces, and there are large prints of 19thC architectural details on the walls. Bathrooms are large and clean, although in one the steps up to the bath could pose a problem for the older visitor. Some rooms have marvellous views on to the piazza, others on to gardens behind. A recent reporter praised 'individual' welcome and service, and the 'calm, comfortable and quiet' atmosphere. They provided 'the best breakfast we have had in Italy' says one reader, although another commented on the wishy-washy coffee. Afternoon tea comes with plenty of biscuits. Five minutes' walk from the Duomo, this hotel is excellent value for money.

∾

NEARBY Church of Santissima Annunziata and San Marco; Accademia museum, Foundlings' Hospital.
LOCATION five minutes' walk N of the Duomo, on W side of Piazza SS Annunziata; garage service on request
FOOD breakfast
PRICE €€€
ROOMS 38 double and twin, 6 single, 4 suites, all with bath or shower; all rooms have phone, TV, radio, safe, air conditioning, minibar, hairdrier
FACILITIES breakfast room, bar
CREDIT CARDS AE, DC, MC, V **DISABLED** not suitable
PETS accepted **CLOSED** never **LANGUAGES** English, French
PROPRIETOR Rodolfo Budini-Gattai

FIRENZE

FLORENCE

MORANDI ALLA CROCETTA

~ TOWN GUESTHOUSE ~

Via Laura 50, 50121 Firenze
TEL (055) 2344747 **FAX** (055) 2480954
E-MAIL hmorandi@dada.it **WEBSITE** www.hotelmorandi.it

MORANDI ALLA CROCETTA, a family-run pensione occupying an apartment in the university part of town in a road leading to Piazza Santissima Annunziata. The entrance looks like any other on the street, without any neon signs, and you must ring a bell to be admitted. Reserve and discretion are the hallmarks here.

Quiet, tasteful interiors greet visitors in the second floor apartment. The polished wooden floors, with strategically placed oriental carpets, echo the beamed ceilings and their decorated corbels. Architectural details are picked out in brick, and the white walls carry only a very few paintings and portraits. There is a small, intimate breakfast room. All is impeccably maintained.

The bedrooms, quiet and comfortable, are furnished with antiques and some well-chosen modern pieces. Two of them have small terraces opening on to a small garden and another has the remains of 17thC frescoes depicting the life and works of Sister Domenica del Paradiso, founder of the original convent. Bathrooms are small but of a high standard. An ideal choice for visitors who need to recover from Florence's stressful centre.

~

NEARBY Santissima Annunziata, San Marco, Baptistry, Duomo.
LOCATION in a quiet street, a few minutes' walk N of the Duomo; pay car parking nearby
FOOD breakfast
PRICE ©©© ©©©
ROOMS 4 double, 2 single, 4 family rooms, all with bath or shower, phone, TV, minibar, safe, central heating, air conditioning, hairdrier
FACILITIES sitting room, breakfast room, bar
CREDIT CARDS AE, DC, MC, V
DISABLED no special facilities **PETS** well-behaved dogs accepted **CLOSED** never
LANGUAGES English, French, German
PROPRIETOR Kathleen Doyle Antuono and family

FIRENZE

FLORENCE

RELAIS MARIGNOLLE
～ COUNTRY VILLA ～

Via di San Quirichino a Marignolle 16, 50124 Firenze
TEL (055) 2286910 **FAX** (055) 2047396 **E-MAIL** relais@marignolle.it
WEBSITE www.marignolle.it

T HE HILLS IMMEDIATELY surrounding Florence are dotted with beautiful properties surrounded by a landscape that belies the fact that only a few kilometres separate them from the chaotic city centre. The Bulleri family have lived in their restored farmhouse set in rambling grounds on a south-facing hillside at Marignolle for some years, but it was only in the summer of 2000 that they opened their converted outbuildings to guests.

On our visit, sun was pouring in through the picture windows of the-large,bright living/breakfast room where comfortable armchairs and sofas, an open fire and an honesty bar encourage one to linger. Bedrooms, while varying in shape and size, are all decorated along the same tasteful lines: stylish country fabrics, padded bed heads, pristine white paintwork and dark parquet floors. The gleaming white bathrooms have large walk-in showers and double basins. Electric kettles (unusual for Italy) and a selection of Antinori wines are supplied in each room. The Bulleris are enthusiastic hosts and will arrange wine tasting tours, golf, shopping trips or even cookery lessons in Signora Bulleri's own kitchen.

～

NEARBY The convent of the Certosa, central Florence (3 km).
LOCATION on a hillside 3 km S of Porta Romana, in own grounds; ample car parking
FOOD breakfast, light lunch on request
PRICE €€€-€€€€
ROOMS 9 doubles and twins, all with shower; all rooms have phone, modem port, TV, air conditioning, mini bar, safe, hairdrier
FACILITIES sitting/breakfast room, gardens, terrace, swimming pool
CREDIT CARDS AE, DC, MC, V
DISABLED no special facilities
PETS not accepted **CLOSED** never
LANGUAGES English, French, German **PROPRIETORS** Bulleri family

FIRENZE

FLORENCE

RELAIS DEGLI UFFIZI
~ TOWN GUESTHOUSE ~

Chiasso de' Baroncelli/Chiasso del Buco, 1650122 Firenze
TEL (055) 2676239 **FAX** (055) 2657909
E-MAIL info@relaisuffizi.it **WEBSITE** www.relaisuffizi.it

IT IS EASY TO GET LOST among the warren of narrow passageways that lead off the south side of Piazza Signoria, and there is no helpful sign to guide you to the Relais degli Uffizi. Look out for a pale stone arch that will lead you to its doorway, through which you'll see, adorning the hall, a pretty lunette fresco of a rooftop scene Make straight for the comfortable sitting room, which has a fabulous view over the piazza. A few minutes of watching the comings and goings in this historic square, sizing up the vast outline of the Palazzo Vecchio, and then pondering the extraordinary silhouette of the cathedral dome to the north will immediately give you a flavour of the city.

The ten bedrooms are arranged on two floors and each is very different from the next. All, however, are tastefully decorated and furnished: pastel colours on the walls, a mix of antique and traditional Florentine painted pieces, and original features such as boxed ceilings, creaky parquet floors and even an enormous fireplace that acts as a bed head (this was the kitchen in the original 16thC house). Several rooms have modern four-poster beds draped with filmy white curtains.

~

NEARBY Ponte Vecchio; Palazzo Vecchio; the Uffizi.
LOCATION in a narrow lane off the south side of Piazza Signoria, with paid car parking nearby
FOOD breakfast
PRICE €€
ROOMS 10 double and twin, 1 single, all with bath or shower; all rooms have phone, TV, air conditioning, minibar, safe, hairdrier
FACILITIES sitting/breakfast room
CREDIT CARDS AE, DC, MC, V **DISABLED** 2 adapted rooms, lift/elevator
PETS accepted if small **CLOSED** never
LANGUAGES English, French, Japanese, Spanish, German
PROPRIETOR Elizabetta Matucci

FIRENZE

FLORENCE

RESIDENZA D'EPOCA
~ TOWN GUESTHOUSE ~

Via dei Magazzini 2, 50123 Firenze
TEL (055) 2399546 **FAX** (055) 2676616
E-MAIL info@inpiazzadellasignoria.com **WEBSITE** www.inpiazzadellasignoria.com

THE BEST BEDROOMS ('Michelangelo' and 'Leonardo') in this smart yet relaxed guesthouse have a full-on view of Piazza Signoria, but most rooms get at least a glimpse of Florence's historic square. Sonia and Alessandro Pini's tall town house dates from the 16th C and is done out in elegant traditional Tuscan style. Each of the ten rooms is different from the next, but there are four-poster and canopied beds, antique furnishings, fine fabrics and oriental rugs on dark parquet floors. Impressive bathrooms are tiled in pale travertine marble; one has a Jacuzzi. Breakfast is served on the third floor at an enormous oval table looking down on to the piazza. Sonia and Alessandro are hands-on hosts and offer a very personal service to their guests with all sorts of thoughtful extras. Fresh flowers abound, the wherewithall for tea and coffee is provided on each floor, and you will be offered a glass of wine or prosecco at aperitivo time. You might even find yourself invited for dinner if they happen to be cooking. There are three sunny, self-catering apartments on the top floor for the independent-minded, and, for the truly adventurous, there is the possibility of chartering the Pinis' yacht, moored near Livorno.

NEARBY Duomo; Palazzo Vecchio; Uffizi; Ponte Vecchio.
LOCATION on narrow street just off Piazza Signoria in a pedestrian area; paid car parking
FOOD breakfast
PRICE €€€
ROOMS 10 doubles and 3 apartments sleeping 4 or 5 with bath or shower; all rooms have phone, TV, safe, air conditioning, hairdrier; the apartments have DVD
FACILITIES breakfast room, bar, lift
CREDIT CARDS AE, DC, MC, V
DISABLED no special facilities
PETS not accepted **CLOSED** never
PROPRIETORS Sonia and Alessandro Pini

FIRENZE

FLORENCE

RESIDENZA JOHLEA UNO
∽ TOWN GUESTHOUSE ∽

Via San Gallo 76, 50129 Firenze
TEL (055) 4633292 **FAX** (055) 4634552
E-MAIL cinquegiornate@johanna.it **WEBSITE** www.johanna.it

IN A CITY WHERE HOTEL PRICES HAVE sky-rocketed over the past few years, it is difficult to believe that a guesthouse can offer three-star comforts at one-star prices, but that's just what the Johlea does. The *residenza* occupies an elegant apartment in a solid *palazzo* just north of the Duomo. The atmosphere is of a gracious private house: indeed, there is no hotel sign on the street and you will be given your own key to come and go. There's no breakfast room either, but rooms are supplied with the wherewithal for a simple breakfast laid out on laquer trays. The bedrooms are stylishly decorated in soft pastel colours and comfortably furnished, partly with antiques. The bathrooms are excellent too.

Upstairs is a cosy little sitting room with an honesty fridge from which guests can help themselves to (and sign for) cold drinks, yoghurts and so on. Up another staircase is the Johlea's crowning glory, a small roof terrace from which there are 360° views of the city. The hotel is situated down the road from the slightly more upmarket Antica Dimora, which is under the same management.

∽

NEARBY Duomo; San Marco; Accademia Gallery.
LOCATION in centre of city, directly north of the duomo; garage parking nearby (extra charge); lift
FOOD breakfast (in room)
PRICE ⓔ
ROOMS 5 double and twin, 1 family, 1 with bath, 5 with shower; all rooms have TV; 3 have air conditioning
FACILITIES sitting room, roof terrace
CREDIT CARDS not accepted
DISABLED no special facilities
PETS accepted
CLOSED never
PROPRIETOR Lea Gulmanelli

FIRENZE

FLORENCE

LE STANZE DI SANTA CROCE
～ TOWN GUESTHOUSE ～

Via delle Pinzochere, 650122 Florence
TEL (055) 2001366 **FAX** (055) 2008456 **E-MAIL** lestanze@viapinzochere6.it
WEBSITE www.viapinzochere6.it / www.cucinareafirenze.it

MARIANGELA CATALANI opened her narrow townhouse to guests in 2002. The location couldn't be better for exploring Florence's art treasures, but foodies will also be well pleased with the vicinity of the bustling Sant' Ambrogio food market, plus a glut of good restaurants and wine bars.

The welcoming, informal reception area is on the first floor and leads to a jasmin-scented terrace where breakfast is served in summer or where guests can relax with something cold from the 'honesty fridge.' The same space is cleverly enclosed in colder weather to make a sunny winter garden. The four bedrooms are all very different, but each has been carefully furnished with a mix of old and new. Pale walls contrast with stronger-coloured fabrics on beds and curtains, while traditional beamed ceilings sit well with contemporary, sometimes quirky, light fittings. One room has a curtained four-poster bed; another (at the top of the house) has skylights and a pale acid green and mauve colour scheme. Mariangela cares about her guests' well-being. She serves delicious dinners on request (by candlelight on the terrace), gives cooking lessons, and is full of useful tips on the area.

～

NEARBY Santa Croce; Sant' Ambrogio market; the Duomo.
LOCATION on a side street off Piazza Santa Croce; paid parking nearby.
FOOD breakfast, dinner on request
PRICE ⓔⓔ
ROOMS 4 double and twin, 3 with shower, 1 with own bathroom (including Jacuzzi); all rooms have phone, air conditioning, hairdrier, safe, modem port
FACILITIES terrace, sitting room
CREDIT CARDS AE, MC, V
DISABLED not suitable
PETS not accepted
CLOSED never **LANGUAGES** English
PROPRIETOR Mariangela Catalani

FIRENZE

FLORENCE

TORNABUONI BEACCI
TOWN GUESTHOUSE

Via Tornabuoni 3, 50123 Firenze
TEL (055) 212645, 268377 **FAX** (055) 283594
E-MAIL info@tornabuonihotels.com **WEBSITE** www.tornabuonihotels.com

ONE COULD NOT ASK for more in terms of location. Via Tornabuoni is one of
Florence's most elegant and central shopping streets, where leading
designers such as Gucci, Ferragamo, Pucci and Prada have their stores,
and all the main sights of the city are within easy walking distance. Yet its
position on the fourth and fifth floors in the 15thC Palazzo Minerbetti
Strozzi, at one corner of Piazza Santa Trinita, makes it a haven from
Florence's crowded, noisy streets.

The *pensione* has a turn-of-the-century atmosphere; fans of E.M.
Forster's *A Room With A View* will find this a close approximation of the
Edwardian guesthouse described in the novel. Many of the rooms have
views, but none so fine as the rooftop terrace, with its plants and pergola,
which looks over the city to the towers and villas of the Bellosguardo hill.
Even in the hot, still days of July and August, you may catch a refreshing
breeze here.

The decoration and furnishings are old-fashioned but well maintained,
like the house of a maiden aunt. Parquet floors and plain covered sofas are
much in evidence. Rooms vary – some are quite poky – but new management has been making improvements.

NEARBY Santa Trinita, Ponte Vecchio, Palazzo della Signoria, Uffizi.
LOCATION in centre of town; car parking in private garage nearby
FOOD breakfast, dinner, snacks (in summer)
PRICE €€€
ROOMS 8 single, 20 double and twin, all with bath or shower; all rooms have
phone, TV, minibar, air conditioning, hairdrier
FACILITIES sitting room, restaurant, roof terrace
CREDIT CARDS AE, DC, MC, V
DISABLED access difficult
PETS small dogs only **CLOSED** never
LANGUAGES English, French, German, Spanish
PROPRIETOR Francesco Bechi

FIRENZE

FLORENCE

TORRE DI BELLOSGUARDO
~ COUNTRY VILLA ~

Via Roti Michelozzi, 250124 Firenze
TEL (055) 2298145**Fax** (055) 229008
E-MAIL Info@Torrebellosguardo.com **WEBSITE** www.torrebellosguardo.com

EVERYBODY HAS HEARD of the hillside of Fiesole, north of Florence, site of the original Etruscan settlement in the area. Less well known, on the southern edge of the city, is the hill of Bellosguardo ('lovely view' in Italian), more discreet in atmosphere and without a busy town to attract trippers. What will draw visitors, however, is this fine hotel – close enough to Florence for easy access but far away enough to guarantee enjoyment of Tuscany's countryside.

As the name suggests, a tower stands at the heart of this 16thC villa, built originally for defence and then surrounded by the trappings of civilization as time passed by. Extraordinary care has been taken to restore the buildings to their former glory after years of abuse as a school in the post-war period. Spacious rooms with painted wood or vaulted ceilings, frescoed walls and the antiques appropriate to the setting create an atmosphere of character and distinction. No two bedrooms are alike and we saw only one that we thought less than admirable. An indoor pool complex incorporating sauna and an underground garage have been built.

~

NEARBY Palazzo Pitti, Boboli gardens and other Florence sights.
LOCATION on the hill of Bellosguardo, just S of the city; underground car parking
FOOD breakfast, lunch
PRICE €€€-€€€€
ROOMS 8 double, 2 single, 6 suites, all with bath; all rooms have phone and central heating; 5 have air conditioning
FACILITIES sitting rooms, breakfast room, bar, garden, indoor swimming pool
CREDIT CARDS AE, MC, V
DISABLED no special facilities
PETS accepted **CLOSED** never
LANGUAGES English, German, French
PROPRIETOR Giovanni Franchetti

FIRENZE

FLORENCE

TORRE GUELFA
~ TOWN BED AND BREAKFAST ~

Borgo SS Apostoli 8, 50123 Firenze
TEL (055) 2396338 **FAX** (055) 2398577 **E-MAIL** torre.guelfa@flashnet.it
WEBSITE www.hoteltorreguelfa.com

THERE CAN BE FEW better spots in Florence in which to enjoy a peaceful *aperitif* after a hard days' sightseeing: this is the tallest privately-owned tower in the city, dating from the 13thC and enjoying a 360° view over a jumble of rooftops, taking in all the most important landmarks and the countryside beyond.

Until now it has been a short entry in this guide, but we're now featuring it as a full page, partly because of its popularity, partly because on viewing it again we thought that the Italian-German owners have created such a relaxing, comfortable and un-stuffy atmosphere, rejecting a heavy, Florentine look for a lighter touch.

Bedroom walls are sponge-painted in pastel shades and curtains are mostly fresh, embroidered white cotton. Furniture is a mixture of wrought iron and prettily painted pieces, with some antiques. Bathrooms are in smart grey Carrara marble.

One room has its own spacious terrace complete with olive tree: be prepared to fight for it. A glassed-in *loggia* makes a sunny breakfast room, and the double 'salon', with its boxed-wood ceiling and little bar, has a comfortable, relaxing atomosphere.

~

NEARBY Ponte Vecchio, Palazzo Vecchio, Palazzo Pitti.
LOCATION in centre of town in traffic limited area; garage parking nearby
FOOD breakfast
PRICE €€€
ROOMS 13 double and twin,1 single, 2 family, all with bath or shower; all rooms have phone, TV, air conditioning, minibar, hairdrier (some)
FACILITIES bar, sitting room, breakfast room, terraces
CREDIT CARDS AE, MC, V
DISABLED one specially adapted room
PETS small ones welcome
CLOSED never **LANGUAGES** English, French, German
PROPRIETOR Giancarlo Avuri

FIRENZE

FLORENCE

VILLA AZALEE
~ TOWN HOTEL ~

Viale Fratelli Rosselli 44, 50123 Firenze
TEL (055) 214242 **FAX** (055) 268264
E-MAIL villaazalee@fi.flashnet.it **WEBSITE** www.villa-azalee.it

CONVENIENT FOR THE STATION but slightly remote from the monumental district (about 15 minutes by foot) Villa Azalee will appeal to visitors who prefer family run hotels with some style to larger, more luxurious operations. And by the standards of most hotels in Florence, prices are very reasonable. The hotel consists of two buildings: the original 19thC villa and, across the garden, a new annexe, full of the potted azaleas that give the place its name.

A highly individual style has been used in the decoration and furniture: some will find the results delightful, others excessively whimsical. Pastel colours, frilly canopies and matching curtains and bed covers characterize the bedrooms. They are all air conditioned, with spotless, new bathrooms. Public rooms are more restrained with an interesting collection of the family's paintings. Breakfast is served either in your room or in the garden (somewhat noisy) or in a separate breakfast room.

One of the drawbacks of the hotel is its location on the *viali* (the busy traffic arteries circling Florence). Soundproofing has been used, but rooms in the annexe, or overlooking the garden, are best. A recent guest commented that it is infinitely nicer than it seems from the outside, and found the staff 'genuinely charming.'

~

NEARBY Santa Maria Novella, Ognissanti, San Lorenzo, Duomo.
LOCATION a few minutes' walk W of the main station, towards Porta al Prato; garage nearby
FOOD breakfast
PRICE €€€
ROOMS 23 double and twin, 2 single, all with bath or shower; all rooms have phone, air conditioning, TV, minibar, hairdrier
FACILITIES sitting room, bar, garden
CREDIT CARDS AE, DC, MC, V
DISABLED 2 adapted rooms **PETS** by arrangement **CLOSED** never
LANGUAGES English, French **PROPRIETOR** Ornella Brizzi

FIRENZE

FLORENCE

VILLA POGGIO SAN FELICE
~ HILLTOP VILLA ~

Via San Matteo in Arcetri 24, 50125 Firenze
TEL (055) 220016 **FAX** (055) 2335388
E-MAIL info@villapoggiosanfelice.com **WEBSITE** www.villapoggiosanfelice.com

THE HILLS IMMEDIATELY to the south of Florence are full of grand and beautiful villas, many of them erstwhile summer residences of wealthy Florentine families. The 15thC Villa Poggio San Felice is such a house; perched on a little *poggio* or hill, it could be in the heart of Chianti but is, in fact, only ten minutes from the city centre. The villa was bought by Gerardo Bernardo Kraft – a Swiss hotelier – in the early 19th century and was recently inherited and restored by his descendants.

The mellow old villa is set in a lovely garden, designed by Porcinai in the late 1800s. Inside, the feeling is very much of an elegant private house, but it is not at all stuffy. Cheerful fabrics and interesting colours give a young feel to the place while blending nicely with family antiques and pictures. The day starts in the long, high-ceilinged breakfast room where French windows open on to the garden. For relaxation, there is a pretty, partially arched *loggia*, plenty of seats dotted around the grounds, or a sitting room for cooler weather. The comfortable and spacious bedrooms – each different from the next – lead off a landing on the first floor, and two have working fireplaces. The suite has a little reading room and a terrace that overlooks the city.

~

NEARBY San Miniato, Piazzale Michelangelo.
LOCATION S of Porta Romana, follow the signs for Arcetri; car parking
FOOD breakfast
PRICE €€€
ROOMS 4 double, 1 twin, 4 with bath, 1 with shower; all rooms have phone; hairdrier on request
FACILITIES sitting room, breakfast room, terraces, garden, free shuttle service to and from Ponte Vecchio
CREDIT CARDS AE, DC, MC, V
DISABLED access difficult **PETS** small pets accepted
CLOSED Jan-Mar
PROPRIETORS Livia Puccinelli and Lorenzo Magnelli

FIRENZE

GREVE IN CHIANTI

VILLA BORDONI
~ COUNTRY VILLA ~

Via San Cresci 31/32, Mezzuola, Greve in Chianti
TEL (055) 8840004 **FAX** (055) 8840005
E-MAIL info@villabordoni.com **WEBSITE** www.villabordoni.com

SCOTTISH RESTAURATEUR David Gardner and his wife Catherine have been well-known on the Florence foodie scene for some years, and their latest venture is this elegant yet relaxed country retreat in the heart of Chianti. They bought the house and grounds in a state of serious decay, but, after a no-expenses-spared restoration, the hotel opened in 2005.

To reach the 19thC patrician villa, immersed in a rolling landscape of vines and olives, you have to negotiate several kilometres of unmetalled road. The interior has been given a stylish, country look using strong, earthy colours, antique furniture, fine fabrics and plenty of attention to detail. A welcoming fire burns in the first floor living room where comfortable sofas and armchairs make tempting spots in which to curl up with a book. The bedrooms vary in shape and size but are all luxurious. Beds are draped with heavy linens and plasma-screen TVs are cleverly disguised as mirrors. Splendid bathrooms have antique tiled floors and showers big enough for a tea party.

Outside, there is a pretty walled Italianate garden, while terraces and the pool area overlook a quintessential Tuscan countryside. Not surprisingly, food is important here: you can sample the chef's excellent take on local dishes in the cosy restaurant. ~

NEARBY Florence (25km), Siena (40 km), Chianti vineyards.
LOCATION Off the SS 222, 5kms west of Greve; in open countryside; ample car parking. NB: make sure you have clear road directions
FOOD breakfast, lunch and dinner
PRICE €€€
ROOMS 6 doubles and 3 suites, one self-catering cottage sleeping 4, all with bath or shower; all rooms have phone, TV, DVD, air conditioning, minibar, hairdrier, safe
FACILITIES sitting room, restaurant, bar, garden, heated pool, gym, mountain bikes
CREDIT CARDS AE, DC, MC, V **DISABLED** no special facilities
CLOSED never
PROPRIETORS David and Catherine Gardner

FIRENZE

VILLA DI VIGNAMAGGIO
~ COUNTRY VILLA ~

Greve in Chianti, 50022 Firenze
TEL (055) 954661 **FAX** (055) 854661
E-MAIL agriturismo@vignamaggio.com **WEBSITE** www.vignamaggio.com

CHIANTI HAS MORE THAN ITS SHARE of hilltop villas and castles, now posing as hotels, or, as in this case, self-catering (*agriturismo*) apartments. Vignamaggio stands out from them all: one of those rare places that made us think twice about advertising it. The villa's first owners were the Gherardini family, of which Mona Lisa, born here in 1479, was a member. This could even have been where she and Leonardo met. More recently, it was the setting for Kenneth Branagh's film of Shakespeare's *Much Ado About Nothing.*

Villa di Vignamaggio is a warm Tuscan pink. A small formal garden in front gives way to acres of vines. The two pools, a short distance from the house, are among fields and trees, and the interior is a perfect combination of simplicity and good taste, with the emphasis on natural materials. Beds, chairs and sofas are comfortable and attractive. Old wardrobes cleverly hide small kitchen units. The three public rooms are equally pleasing, and breakfast there or on the terrace is thoughtfully planned, with bread from the local bakery and home-made jam. The staff were charming and helpful when we visited. 'Service' is kept to a minimum ("This is not a hotel"). It is possible to have a guided tour of the cellars and taste wine.

~

NEARBY Greve (5 km); Florence (19 km); Siena (38 km).
LOCATION 5 km SE of Greve on the road to Lamole from the SS222; car parking
FOOD breakfast; dinner 2 evenings a week
PRICE €€
ROOMS 21 rooms, suites, self-catering apartments for 2-4, all with bath; all rooms/apartments have phone, air conditioning
FACILITIES sitting room, bar, terrace, garden, 2 swimming pools, gym, tennis court, children's playground, billiards room, Turkish bath, range of beauty treatments
CREDIT CARDS AE, MC, V
DISABLED one specially adapted apartment
PETS accepted **CLOSED** mid Nov-mid Mar
LANGUAGES English, German, French **PROPRIETOR** Gianni Nunziante

FIRENZE

SALVADONICA
~ COUNTRY GUESTHOUSE ~

Via Grevigiana 82, 50024 Mercatale Val di Pesa, Firenze
TEL (055) 8218039 **FAX** (055) 8218043
E-MAIL info@salvadonica.com **WEBSITE** www.salvadonica.com

Two enterprising sisters have turned their family's 14thC farm properties into a thriving guesthouse and apartment complex. Set in rolling countryside, south of Florence, this conversion has been carried out with style and panache, exploiting the buildings' character and position to the maximum. The central house is a warm pink and is surrounded by stone farmhouses with their details picked out in brick. In the paved courtyard stands a single umbrella pine. The enthusiasm of Francesca and Beatrice and their friendly welcome makes for a vivacious, friendly atmosphere.

Elegance and comfort characterize the rooms and apartments, with individual variations on the classic rustic ingredients of beamed ceilings, simple white plaster walls and warm, terracotta-tiled floors. A particularly impressive apartment with refined brick vaulting and columns looks more like the crypt of a Renaissance church than a converted cow byre. With a swimming pool, tennis court and riding (nearby) as well as easy access to Tuscany's most important art cities, your stay at Salvadonica will seem all too short. A recent visitor was thoroughly enchanted.

NEARBY Florence (20 km); Siena (40 km).
LOCATION 20 km S of Florence, E of road to Siena; own grounds, car parking
FOOD breakfast, snacks
PRICE €€€
ROOMS 5 double, 10 apartments, all with bath or shower; all rooms have phone, apartments have fridge
FACILITIES breakfast room, garden, swimming pool, billiards, tennis, play area
CREDIT CARDS AE, DC, MC, V
DISABLED two adapted rooms
PETS if small (extra charge) **CLOSED** Nov-Feb
LANGUAGES English, German
PROPRIETORS Beatrice and Francesca Baccetti

FIRENZE

IL BORGHETTO
~ COUNTRY VILLA ~

Via Collina 23, Montefiridolfi, S. Casciano Val di Pesa, 50020 Firenze
TEL (055) 0244442 **FAX** (055) 8244247
E-MAIL info@borghetto.org **WEBSITE** www.borghetto.org

DISCRETION, TASTE AND REFINEMENT are the key characteristics of this family guesthouse, much appreciated by a discerning (and returning) clientèle that enjoys civilized living in a peaceful, bucolic setting.

A manicured gravel drive, with rose beds and cypress trees, leads past the lawn to the main buildings, which include the remains of two 15thC military towers. From a covered terrace, where breakfast is accompanied by views of miles of open countryside, a broad-arched entrance leads to the open-plan ground floor of the main villa. Within, the usual starkness of the Tuscan style has been softened by the use of muted tones in the wall colours and fabrics. Comfortable furniture abounds without cluttering the spacious, airy quality of the public areas. Upstairs, in the bedrooms (some of which are not particularly large), floral wallpaper and subdued lighting create a balmy, relaxed atmosphere. No intrusive phone calls or blaring televisions.

Even the refined like a swim; but for those who consider swimming pools raucous, there is a soothing water garden.

Cookery courses are organized here at certain times of the year.

~

NEARBY Florence (18 km); Siena (45 km); San Gimignano (40 km).
LOCATION 18 km S of Florence, E of Siena road, on right before village; car parking
FOOD breakfast; lunch and dinner if sufficient numbers request
PRICE €€€ (2 day min. stay)
ROOMS 6 doubles, 2 suites, all with shower
FACILITIES sitting room, dining room, terrace, gardens, swimming pool
CREDIT CARDS not accepted
DISABLED one suitable room with bathroom
PETS not accepted
CLOSED Nov-Mar
LANGUAGES English, French, German
PROPRIETOR Antonio Cavallini

FIRENZE

PANZANO IN CHIANTI

VILLA LE BARONE
∼COUNTRY VILLA ∼

Via San Leolino 19, Panzano in Chianti,, 50020 Firenze
TEL (055) 852621 **FAX** (055) 852277
E-MAIL villalebarone.it **WEBSITE** info@villalebarone.it

ONE OF THE GREAT DELIGHTS of aristocrats finding their villas too large and expensive to run is that, when they retire to the tastefully converted chicken house, they leave behind them family collections of antiques, paintings and *objets d'art*, painstakingly put together over the centuries, which no interior decorator could hope to imitate. Such is the case with Le Barone, a small gem of a villa. Now owned by Count Corso and Countess Jacqueline Aloisi de Larderel, who take a keen interest in their inheritance.

An air of unforced refinement and aristocratic ease in a setting of withdrawn tranquillity will immediately strike any visitor. The public rooms are small in scale and slightly cluttered; in the sitting room, with its blue and yellow sofas, dominated at one end by a carved-stone fireplace, there is a collection of family paintings and books which you are welcome to read. The bar, where you help yourself and write it down in a book, has seats made from wine barrels. Every two weeks there is a free wine-tasting, run by different local vineyards, on the terrace before dinner. The gardens are a delight, full of roses and olives, and the owners have researched four local walks (the details of which are provided in an informative information pack available in every room). One reader comments that is the kind of place that attracts people who return year after year.

∼

NEARBY Greve (6 km); Florence (31 km); Siena (31 km).
LOCATION 6 km S of Greve; car parking
FOOD breakfast, lunch, dinner, snacks
PRICE €€€
ROOMS 28 double and twin, 22 with bath, 6 with shower, 1 single with shower; all rooms have phone, hairdrier, 15 have air conditioning
FACILITIES 3 sitting rooms, TV room, self-service bar, dining room, breakfast room, swimming pool, tennis court, table tennis, internet wi-fi conneection point
CREDIT CARDS AE, MC, V **DISABLED** ground floor rooms **PETS** not accepted
CLOSED Nov-Mar **PROPRIETOR** Count and Countess Aloisi de Larderel

FIRENZE

PANZANO IN CHIANTI

VILLA ROSA
~ COUNTRY GUESTHOUSE ~

Via S. Leolino 59, Panzano in Chianti, Firenze
TEL (055) 852577 **FAX** (055) 8560835 **E-MAIL** villa.rosa@flashnet.it
WEBSITE www.resortvillarosa.com

A RECENT ADDITION to the countless hotels and guest houses in this part of Chianti, Villa Rosa is a solid structure dating from the early 1900s. Looming over the road from Panzano to Radda, its appearance makes a refreshing change form the usual rustic stone Tuscan farmhouse formula: it is painted bright pink.

Inside, a light touch is evident in the the decoration. The terracotta floors and white walls downstairs are typical, but bedrooms have pastel-coloured, sponged paintwork, wrought iron four-poster beds and a mixture of wicker furniture, together with antique pieces here and there. The attractive, rather quirky, light fittings are by a local craftsman. Bathrooms also have touches of colour while heated towel rails add a hint of luxury.

The building is too near the road to be ideally situated, but at the back there is a peaceful, partially shaded terrace for outdoor eating, while the garden slopes up the hillside to a pleasant pool and open, vine-striped countryside. Reasonable prices and a relaxed style of management make this hotel very popular; the food is good, too. A recent report remarks on the 'interesting local fare', and comments that the place is 'good value'.

~

NEARBY Florence (34 km); Siena (28 km).
LOCATION 3 km SE of Panzano on Radda road; car parking
FOOD breakfast, dinner
PRICE (€)
ROOMS 16 double and twin with bath or shower; all rooms have phone, TV, minibar
FACILITIES garden, terraces, sitting room, restaurant, swimming pool
CREDIT CARDS AE, MC, V
DISABLED one specially adapted room, but access difficult
PETS accepted
CLOSED mid Nov-just before Easter
LANGUAGES English, French, German
PROPRIETOR Sabine Buntenbach

FIRENZE

PANZANO IN CHIANTI

VILLA SANGIOVESE
~ COUNTRY VILLA ~

Piazza Bucciarelli 5, 50020 Panzano in Chianti, Firenze
TEL (055) 852461 **FAX** (055) 852463
E-MAIL villa.sangiovese@libero.it **WEBSITE** www.wel.it/villasangiovese

THE BLEULERS ONCE MANAGED the long-established Tenuta di Ricavo at Castellina (page 118). They opened their doors in Panzano, a few miles to the north, in 1988 after completely renovating the building, and winning high praise from our readers.

The main villa is a neat stone and stucco house fronting directly on to a back street; potted plants and a brass plate beside the doorway are the only signs of a hotel. Attached to this house is an old rambling stone building beside a flowery, gravelled courtyard-terrace offering splendid views. The landscaped garden below includes a fair sized pool.

Inside, all is mellow, welcoming and stylish, with carefully chosen antique furnishings against plain, pale walls. Bedrooms, some with wood-beamed ceilings are spacious, comfortably, and tastefully restrained in decoration. The dining room is equally simple and stylish, with subdued wall lighting and bentwood chairs on a tiled floor.

A limited but interestng *á la carte* menu is offered, which changes each night, and service is on the terrace in summer. A recent reporter praised the food and the wine.

~

NEARBY Greve (5 km); Siena (30 km); Florence (30 km).
LOCATION on edge of town, 5 km S of Greve; car parking
FOOD breakfast, lunch, dinner
PRICE €€
ROOMS 16 double, 1 single, 2 suites, all with bath or shower; all rooms have phone, rooms facing the *piazza* have air conditioning, TV on request
FACILITIES dining room, 2 sitting rooms, library, bar, terrace, swimming pool
CREDIT CARDS MC, V **DISABLED** no special facilities
PETS not accepted
CLOSED 15 Dec-end Feb; restaurant Wed
MANAGERS Ulderico and Anna Maria Bleuler

FIRENZE

PELAGO

LA DOCCIA
~ COUNTRY GUESTHOUSE ~

19-20 Ristonchi, 50060 Pelago, Firenze
TEL (055) 8361387 **FAX** (055) 8361388
E-MAIL ladoccia@tin.it **WEBSITE** www.ladocciawelcomes.com

EDWARD AND SONIA MAYHEW opened their beautifully converted stone farmhouse to guests in May 1999. Stunningly situated high up in the hills in a refreshingly undiscovered corner of Tuscany, the style is comfortable rustic with handmade terracotta flagstones, beamed ceilings, stone staircases and brick arches. Warm colours on the walls make a welcome change from the usual stark white. The furniture is a successful mix of locally made pieces and the Mayhews' own English antiques, while books, pictures on the walls and knick-knacks give it the feel of a private house. This style is continued in the comfortable bedrooms and self-contained apartments, which are carefully furnished and have particularly smart bathrooms; two of the apartments have open fires for added cosiness in winter.

There are two sitting rooms, both with fireplaces (one is enormous), and an honesty bar. Breakfast and dinner (the latter prepared by Edward) are served at a long communal table. The house stands at 630 metres above sea level, so the long stone terrace, shaded by large, white umbrellas and bordered by lavender and roses, has fabulous views over the hills and down to Florence far below. 2006 sees the addition of a smart pool.

NEARBY Florence (27 km); Vallombrosa (8 km).
LOCATION 27 km E of Florence, 5 km S of Pelago; car parking
FOOD breakfast; lunch and dinner by arrangement
PRICE ⓔⓔ
ROOMS 5 double, 4 apartments for 2-4 people, all with bath or shower
FACILITIES sitting rooms, dining room, bar, terraces, garden, swimming pool
CREDIT CARDS AE, MC, V
DISABLED no special facilities
PETS accepted
CLOSED B & B rooms Dec-Feb; apartments never
PROPRIETORS Edward and Sonia Mayhew

FIRENZE

REGELLO

VILLA RIGACCI
~ HILLTOP VILLA ~

Vággio 76, Regello 50066, Firenze
TEL (055) 865 6718 **FAX** (055) 865 6537
E-MAIL hotel@villarigacci.it **WEBSITE** www.villarigacci.com

THIS CREEPER-COVERED 15thC farmhouse stands in a beautiful secluded spot – a hill-top surrounded by olive groves, pines, chestnut trees and meadows – yet only a few kilometres from the Florence-Rome autostrada and a short drive from Florence and Arezzo.

The house achieves a cosy and relaxed atmosphere in spite of its four-star facilities. It is furnished as a cherished family home, much of it reflecting Signor Pierazzi's Camargue background, including some lovely antiques from the region and prints of Camargue horses. Bedrooms – the best are gloriously spacious and full of gleaming antiques – overlook the gardens and tranquil swimming pool.

The sitting room has an open fire in chilly weather; the breakfast room is a converted stable with the hay racks still on the walls. The elegantly rustic dining room offers local, Italian and French-influenced dishes. Guests are well cared for – if you are peckish, for example, you can order snacks or light meals at any time of the day. In summer, fish and meat are cooked al fresco on the large outdoor barbecue. Next to the house is a tiny family chapel where Mass is still occasionally said.

~

NEARBY Florence (35 km); Arezzo (45 km).
LOCATION 300 m N of Vággio, 30 km SE of Florence; exit Incisa from A1; with car parking and shady, tree-filled gardens
FOOD breakfast, lunch, dinner
PRICE €€€
ROOMS 3 single, 15 double, 4 suites; all with bath and shower, TV, minibar, air conditioning, heating, phone
FACILITIES sitting room, restaurant, bar, terrace, garden, pool
CREDIT CARDS AE, DC, MC, V
DISABLED no special facilities **PETS** accepted **CLOSED** never
LANGUAGES English, German, French, Spanish, Arabic
PROPRIETORS Federico Pierazzi

FIRENZE

SESTO FIORENTINO

VILLA VILLORESI
~ TOWN VILLA ~

Via Campi 2, Colonnata di Sesto Fiorentino, 50019 Firenze
TEL (055) 443212 **FAX** (055) 442063
E-MAIL ILAVilloresi@ila-chateau.com **WEBSITE** www.ila-chateau.com/villoresi

THE ARISTOCRATIC VILLA VILLORESI looks rather out of place in what is now an industrial suburb of Florence, but once in the house and gardens you suddenly feel a million miles away from modern, bustling Florence. Contessa Cristina Villoresi is a warm hostess who has captured the hearts of many transatlantic and other guests. It is thanks to her that the villa still has the feel of a private home – all rather grand, if a little faded and standing still in time.

As you make your way through the building, each room seems to have some curiosity or feature of the past. The entrance hall is a superb gallery of massive chandeliers, frescoed walls, antiques and lofty potted plants. Then there is the first-floor loggia, the longest in Tuscany, on to which five of the finest bedrooms open. Another, on the ground floor, has crystal chandeliers, floor-to-ceiling frescoes, and a canopied bed. Other bedrooms, however, are very different: small and plain with simple painted furniture, and looking on to an inner courtyard.

In the two dining rooms Tuscan specialities are served. Contessa Villoresi runs residential courses on the Italian Renaissance.

~

NEARBY Florence (8 km).
LOCATION 9 km NW of Florence; adequate parking
FOOD breakfast, lunch, dinner
PRICE €€-€€€
ROOMS 23 double, 5 single; all rooms have bath, shower, TV on request, heating, phone
FACILITIES sitting rooms, restaurant, bar, terraces, garden, pool, walks
CREDIT CARDS AE, DC, MC, V
DISABLED ground floor rooms
PETS not in public rooms
CLOSED never
LANGUAGES English, German, French
PROPRIETOR Contessa Cristina Villoresi

FIRENZE

VICCHIO

VILLA CAMPESTRI
∼ COUNTRY HOTEL ∼

Via di Campestri 19/22, Vicchio di Mugello, 50039 Firenze
TEL (055) 8490107 **FAX** (055) 8490108
E-MAIL villa.campestri@villacampestri.it **WEBSITE** www.villacampestri.it

MUGELLO IS THE NAME of the little-visited area north-east of Florence characterized by dramatic mountain landscapes bordering wide river valleys. Wilder than Chianti, it is increasingly frequented by Florentines in search of unspoilt countryside without the bill-boards that are becoming eyesores in the more popular parts of Tuscany. Unfortunately, you will not find too many decent hotels either, and Villa Campestri is by far the most stylish in the area.

The Renaissance villa, a square, imposing building in off-white stucco, stands on top of a hill in open countryside. Before being turned into a hotel it was owned by the same family for over six hundred years. Much of its former grandeur remains: on the ground floor, stately public rooms paved in stone or dark terracotta are hung with faded tapestries and oil paintings. One of them has fine stained windows executed by Chini in Liberty style. The restaurant is one of the best in the area. (It is also a popular place for wedding parties, which can be a nuisance at weekends.) Bedrooms are equally grand in the villa, though a few more homely ones have been added in the next-door farmhouse. The proprietor, Paolo, has his own olive press, so should you go at olive picking time (November), you can see the oil being made. He is considered to be one of Tuscany's olive oil experts.

∼

NEARBY Florence (35 km).
LOCATION 3 km S of Vicchio, in own grounds; ample car parking
FOOD breakfast, dinner, snacks
PRICE €€€–€€€€
ROOMS 14 double, 6 suites, 1 single, all with bath or shower, phone, satellite TV, minibar
FACILITIES sitting rooms, restaurant, bar, swimming pool, horse riding; golf nearby
CREDIT CARDS MC, V **DISABLED** 4 adapted rooms **PETS** small dogs, only on request
CLOSED Jan-Mar **LANGUAGES** English **PROPRIETOR** Paolo Pasquali

FIRENZE

IL PALAZZACCIO
VILLA APARTMENTS

Via Vicinale di Paterno 3,
Bagno a Ripoli, 50012 Firenze

TEL (055) 630127
FAX (055) 630301
E-MAIL none **FOOD** self-catering
PRICE € **CLOSED** never

ON THE HILLS of the little town of Bagno a Ripoli, just 9 km south-east of Florence, stands this elegant privately owned villa, dating from the 15th century with toffee-coloured walls and green shutters along its symmetrical sides. All around is a shady ornamental garden, approached via gravel paths, with pillared pergolas, low-hedged parterres and lemon and orange trees in vast old terracotta pots. Beyond that, a discreetly tiled swimming pool with a surprise in store: a view across the landscape of Brunelleschi's great cupola on the Duomo. The five self-catering apartments, sleeping between four and eight people each, are stylish and fully equipped. A bus service will take you to the centre of Florence.

LA SPINOSA
FARM BED AND BREAKFAST

Via Le Masse 8, Barberino Val
d'Elsa, 50021 Firenze

TEL (055) 8075413
FAX (055) 8066214
E-MAIL info@laspinosa.it
WEBSITE www.laspinosa.it
FOOD breakfast, lunch, dinner
PRICE €€
CLOSED never

A GENUINE WORKING FARM now run on strict macrobiological principles by a team of five without the use of herbicides or insecticides. The stone-built farmhouse has been decorated and furnished with considerable care and taste (apart from some garish fitted carpets) You are unlikely to get bored here: as well as the swimming pool and tennis court, there is a rural park where you can walk or bird-watch, and its latest project - a country theatre. There is a tradition of plays and musical diversions being staged in inns that stretches back to the Middle Ages, and with its 'Il Piccolo Teatro del Carbone', La Spinosa offers a 21stC version as entertainment for its guests.

FIRENZE

CERTALDO

OSTERIA DEL VICARIO

TOWN HOTEL

*Via Rivellino 3, Certaldo Alto,
50052 Firenze*

TEL (055) 668228
E-MAIL info@osteriadelvicario.it
FOOD breakfast, lunch, dinner
PRICE €-€€
CLOSED Jan (restaurant Wed)

CERTALDO ALTO IS A SMALL but fascinating medieval town, not least because it was the home of Boccaccio. Next to the Podesta is Osteria del Vicario, occupying a former monastery which dates from the 13th century and has for more than 50 years offered creative Tuscan cooking in the characterful dining room. Summer meals are served in the delightful pebble garden, which was once the monastery's cloister, and has views across the surrounding countryside. As for the series of bedrooms, some in the main building, others in two nearby townhouses, they are well-kept and carefully furnished, with rich colours for fabrics, antique furnishings and beamed ceilings, well worth a stay of a night or two.

CORTINE

FATTORIA CASA SOLA

COUNTRY APARTMENTS

*Cortine, Barberino Val d'Elsa,
50021 Firenze*

TEL & FAX (055) 8075028
E-MAIL
casasola@chianticlassico.com
FOOD dinner on request
PRICE €-€€ CLOSED never

MONTARSICCIO, ONE OF THE OLD farmhouses on the Casa Sola estate (which produces Chianti, olive oil and vin santo) has been pleasantly converted to apartments in classic Tuscan rustic style, each with its own garden area and access to the pool beside the main villa. The farm in is the heart of the Chianti Classico Gallo Nero area midway between Florence and Siena, with a mix of vineyards and olive groves. The six apartments each have individual entrances and verandas, and provide good family accommodation. Guests are offered guided tours of the *fattoria*, as well as wine tastings and Tuscan-style lunches and dinners in the dining room. Swimming pool, riding and mountain bikes.

FIRENZE

FIESOLE

FATTORIA DI MAIANO

COUNTRY APARTMENTS

Via da Maiano 11, Fiesole, Firenze

TEL (055) 599600
FAX (055) 599640 **E-MAIL**
maiano@contemiarifulcis.it
FOOD self-catering
PRICE € (heating not included)
CLOSED never

ONLY 5 KM FROM Florence's centre, but, aside from the view (familiar to those who have seen the film *A Room with a View*) you could be in deep countryside. Classily furnished rustic apartments in farmhouses that surround an imposing villa with beautiful gardens (once a cloistered convent), they form part of a 15thC hamlet on one of Tuscany's only organic olive oil farms. There's a small swimming pool, and a shop that sells the estate's own produce. The estate runs cooking and decorative arts courses and group tours of the villa, which is owned by Countess Lucrezia Corsini Miari Fulcis.

FLORENCE

BOTTICELLI

TOWN HOTEL

Via Taddea 8, 50123 Firenze

TEL (055) 290905
FAX (055) 294322
E-MAIL info@hotelbotticelli.it
WEBSITE
www.panoramahotelsitlay.it
FOOD breakfast
PRICE €€
CLOSED never

OCCUPYING TWO *'palazzi'* (one dating from the 1500s with a frescoed, vaulted ceiling in the entrance), the Botticelli is near bustling San Lorenzo market. The bedrooms (some rather poky) are comfortable and modern, but original architectural features have been preserved where possible. Furnishings are refined. Guests approve of its convenient location, great staff, and low-key charm; but one U.S. traveller warns of not enough closet space in a bedroom.

FIRENZE

FLORENCE

CASCI
TOWN HOTEL

Via Cavour 13, 50129 Firenze

TEL (055) 211686
FAX (055) 2396461
E-MAIL info@hotelcasci.com
WEBSITE www.hotelcasci.com
FOOD breakfast
PRICE €-€€
CLOSED never

THOUGH EXTREMELY CLOSE to the Duomo and Palazzo Medici-Riccardi (a prototype of Renaissance and Baroque architecture) in a 15thC *palazzo* that once belonged to the composer Rossini, this pleasant hotel stands on Via Cavour which, it must be said, is one of the city's main bus arteries. So, notwithstanding the sound-proofing, ask for a quiet room at the back. The Casci is family-run and it shows: there's always a welcoming atmosphere and a reader reports that the 'owners do all they can to ensure a comfortable stay for their guests'. Rooms are clean, with air conditioning, safes and fridges, and there is a useful free internet access point in the lobby. The breakfast room and the bar have frescoed ceilings.

FLORENCE

DESIREE
TOWN HOTEL

Via Fiume 20, 50123 Firenze

TEL (055) 2382382
FAX (055) 291439
E-MAIL info@desireehotel.com
WEBSITE www.desireehotel.com
FOOD breakfast
PRICE €-€€
CLOSED never

CLOSE TO THE STATION, which is convenient but not without its occasional disadvantages, the Desiree has 18 rooms, but still feels like a small *pensione*. It is carefully managed by its owners, who have decided on a clean, simple approach with occasional touches of style such as patterned tiled floors. Several of the rooms look out on to Florence's chaotic rooftops, and the pleasant breakfast room has a view. However, there have been several reports of noise at night, and rooms at the back of the hotel are recommended. Friendly, helpful staff.

FIRENZE

FLORENCE

MONNA LISA
TOWN HOTEL

Borgo Pinti 27, 50121 Firenze

TEL (055) 2479751
FAX (055) 2479755
E-MAIL monnalis@ats.it
WEBSITE www.monnalisa.it
FOOD breakfast
PRICE €€€-€€€€
CLOSED never

THE ENTRANCE, at the back of a covered area opening into the palazzo from Borgo Pinti, is as discreet as the hotel itself. It's an intriguing place, the maze of rooms on the ground floor have Doric and Corinthian columns supporting heavy, decorated wooden ceilings. Light floods in from the back through leaded windows giving on to the garden. Old terracotta floors, dark and shiny from centuries of wax polish, lead the eye from one room to another. The family's collection of paintings give a pleasant, cluttered feel to the public spaces. The garden is a definite plus, and breakfast is served here in fine weather. Some of the bedrooms have small terraces overlooking the green haven. Reports especially welcome.

FLORENCE

ORTO DEI MEDICI
TOWN HOTEL

Via San Gallo 30, 50129 Firenze

TEL (055) 483427
E-MAIL hotel@ortodeimedici.it
WEBSITE www.ortodeimedici.it
FOOD breakfast
PRICE €€€-€€€€
CLOSED never

THE FORMER HOTEL SPLENDOUR has transmogrified into the Hotel Orto dei Medici, but despite the name change not much else is different. Close to the Piazza San Marco, it's a surprisingly swish place for the price, where you will find frescoed ceilings and chandeliers, marble busts and hand-painted walls. The first floor breakfast room, where a copious buffet is served, has elegant painted panels and floor to ceiling windows on to the sunny terrace, from where, under white umbrellas, you can see across to the monastery of San Marco, its monks' cells decorated by Fra Angelico. Bedrooms are standardized, with ubiquitous brocade bedspreads and reproduction furnishings.

FIRENZE

FLORENCE

PALAZZO DEL BORGO
TOWN HOTEL

Via della Scala 6, 50123 Firenze

TEL (055) 216237
FAX (055) 280947
E-MAIL info@hotelaprile.it
FOOD breakfast, snacks
PRICE €€-€€€
CLOSED never

THIS COMPACT TOWN HOTEL used to be called simply Hotel Aprile, but recently, although under the same ownership as before, it has added the name Palazzo del Borgo, which is what the building was called in Medici times, when it was constructed on a street leading away from Piazza Santa Maria Novella. To be frank, the hotel could make more of its architectural inheritance than merely changing its name, but still there are vaulted ceilings, a shady courtyard (always a bonus in Florence) and views from some of the bedrooms, all of which have now been renovated, of the church of Santa Maria Novella. Prices have hardly risen, and it makes a very comfortable base in Florence.

THE REGENCY
TOWN HOTEL

Piazza Massimo d'Azeglio 3, 50121 Firenze

TEL (055) 245247
FAX (055) 2346735
E-MAIL info@regency-hotel.com
WEBSITE www.regency-hotel.com
FOOD breakfast, lunch, dinner
PRICE €€€€
CLOSED never

A FIFTEEN TO TWENTY-MINUTE walk along busy, traffic clogged streets from the centre of Florence, the Regency's location slightly outside the hub is somewhat to its disadvantage, though its cool and shady garden is a definite plus, and you can dine on a veranda overlooking it. The dining room of restaurant Le Jardin, well known for its sophisticated cooking, is resplendent with grandiose mirrors, boiserie and antique, hand-painted stained glass. Some might find the opulent style of decoration (not just in the dining room) rather overwhelming, although it is undeniably luxurious. Originally constructed for high government officials and ministers of State, the hotel overlooks neat Piazza d'Azeglio. The intimate sitting rooms and bedrooms are as traditionally smart as you might imagine.

FIRENZE

FLORENCE

LA RESIDENZA
TOWN HOTEL

Via Tornabuoni 8, 50123 Firenze

TEL (055) 284197
FAX (055) 284197
E-MAIL info@laresidenzahotel.com
FOOD breakfast, dinner
PRICE €-€€
CLOSED never

VIA TORNABUONI is one of the most fashionable shopping streets in Italy, if not in Europe, where the price of a pair of shoes would cover five nights stay at La Residenza. So do not expect anything particularly chic, (some reports describe it as 'shabby'), but enjoy the quirky, friendly atmosphere, the flowery roof terrace (with views across a jumble of tiled rooftops) and simple value-for-money accommodation. The building dates back to the 14thC and has been owned by the Giacalone family for two generations, who - as reporters confirm - succeed in giving it a winning, personal touch.

FLORENCE

SILLA
TOWN GUESTHOUSE

Via dei Renai 5, 50125 Firenze

TEL (055) 2342888
FAX (055) 2341437
E-MAIL hotelsilla@tin.it
WEBSITE www.hotelsilla.it
FOOD breakfast
PRICE €€-€€€
CLOSED 2 weeks in Dec

AN EXCELLENT LOCATION in the quiet residential, medieval area of San Niccolo south of the Arno, but ten minutes' walk of the main sights. This old-fashioned family-owned pensione occupies the first floor of a 16thC *palazzo* and from its terrace you can see Florence's famous skyline. Readers have endorsed it again this year, commenting particularly on the 'clean, spacious' rooms (with air conditioning and minibars) and 'lovely terrace facing the Arno'. Public rooms are calm and elegant, but the busy wallpaper in the bedrooms will not be to everyone's taste.

FIRENZE

FLORENCE

VILLA BELVEDERE

SUBURBAN HOTEL

*Via Benedetto Castelli 3, 50124
Firenze*

TEL (055) 222501/502
E-MAIL reception@villa-belvedere.com
FOOD breakfast, snacks
PRICE ©©-©©©
CLOSED Dec-Feb

HARDLY AN ARCHITECTURAL GEM, but a pleasant place to retreat to after a day's trekking around the city. Situated on the hill of Poggio Imperiale, beyond the old city gate of Porta Romana, surrounded by trees in well-kept gardens (with a pool and tennis court) and with views of the town, it has been thoroughly recommended by a number of recent guests. Of particular note are the 'immaculate, clean, large rooms', filled with 'fresh flowers', beds with 'good mattresses and fine bed-linen', 'courteous staff' and 'excellent breakfasts'. Interiors are modern and comfortable without being exciting.

FLORENCE

VILLA LIBERTY

TOWN HOTEL

*Viale Michelangiolo 40, 50125
Firenze*

TEL (055) 6810581
FAX (055) 6812595
E-MAIL info@hotelvillaliberty.com
FOOD breakfast
PRICE ©©©
CLOSED never

TURN-OF-THE-CENTURY VILLA with remnants of the Art Deco style of the period – decorated mirrors, stained glass, wrought ironwork and ornate lamps. The best bedrooms have exposed beams or high frescoed ceilings. It is located some distance from the city centre in an attractive area of small shops and restaurants, with an appealing shady garden and tennis courts just 150m away. There is also a snack bar and a private garage. Ask for a room on the garden side: at weekends, Viale Michelangiolo is busy until the small hours. Some recent visitors complain of unfriendly service and poor maintenance. More reports please.

FIRENZE

LA FATTORESSA

FARM GUESTHOUSE

*Via Volterrana 58, Galluzzo,
50124 Firenze*

TEL & FAX (055) 2048418
E-MAIL fattoressa@intervos.com
FOOD breakfast
PRICE (€)
CLOSED never

CONVENIENT IF YOU WANT to be close enough to Florence for day visits, but prefer to spend evenings in country surroundings. Rooms, available in the old *casa colonica* (farmhouse) and converted outbuildings, are simply furnished, clean and comfortable. Bus nearby goes to the centre, avoiding Florence's nightmare car parking. La Fattoressa is a working farm, serving its produce at the communal dining table, and is run in hands-on style by the friendly and energetic Signora Fusi. It is close to the magnificent Carthusian monastery of Galluzzo.

LA CAMPORENA

FARM GUESTHOUSE

*Via Figlinese 27, Greve in
Chianti, 50022 Firenze*

TEL (055) 853184, 8544765
FAX (055) 8544784 **E-MAIL**
ritouristanna@lacamporena.com
FOOD breakfast, dinner
PRICE (€) **CLOSED** never

ALSO KNOWN AS Agriturismo Anna, located 3 km outside Greve on the road to Figline. A tree-lined drive leads up to this hilltop farmhouse, a position both peaceful and panoramic with views across the surrounding olive groves and vineyards, where the grapes that make the famous Chianti Classico Gallo Nero are grown. It is still a working farm, and the house is decorated in an appropriately down-to-earth fashion, with plain walls and country furniture. Simple, cheap accommodation, with access to a pleasant garden, terrace, swimming pool and with a restaurant that serves home-made regional food.

FIRENZE

CASTELLO VICCHIOMAGGIO

CONVERTED CASTLE

Greve in Chianti, 50022 Firenze

TEL (055) 854079
FAX (055) 853911
WEBSITE www.vicchiomaggio.it
FOOD breakfast, lunch, dinner
PRICE €-€€€ **CLOSED** never

THIS ANCIENT HILLTOP castle on a famous wine estate overlooks a landscape of vines, olive and cypress trees and is owned and run by John and Paola Matta. It is one of Tuscany's most historic and best-preserved castles whose origins can be traced back to the 5thC. Inside, the dimensions are impressive and possibly rather impersonal, and this goes also for the self-catering apartments. There is also a huge dining room with vaulted ceilings, and it's not difficult to imagine Leonardo da Vinci as a guest here (he stayed in the castle whilst he was painting the 'Mona Lisa'). A formal Italian-style garden together with a pool which has a glorious view, are bonuses.

ALBERGO DEL CHIANTI

TOWN HOTEL

Piazza G. Matteotti 86, Greve in Chianti, 50022 Firenze

TEL (055) 853763
FAX (055) 853764
E-MAIL info@albergodelchianti
FOOD breakfast, lunch, dinner
PRICE € **CLOSED** Nov

A FRIENDLY ATMOSPHERE and an enticing swimming pool are the main attractions of this simple hotel, located in Greve's principal piazza. The large entrance acts as reception, bar, sitting area and breakfast room. Decent Tuscan food is served in the more traditionally styled trattoria or on the back terrace. Bedrooms aren't quite all the same, but furnishings, though inoffensive, are somewhat standardized. Greve, about equidistant (25 km) from Siena and Florence, is considered to be the capital of the Chianti wine region and makes a particularly good base for a wine holiday: it hosts exhibitions, markets and fairs.

FIRENZE

IL BURCHIO

FARMHOUSE CLUB

*Via Poggio al Burchio 4, Incisa
Valdarno, 50064 Firenze*

TEL (055) 8330124
FAX (055) 8330234
E-MAIL none
WEBSITE www.ilburchio.com
FOOD breakfast , lunch, dinner
PRICE €-€€
CLOSED end Oct-end Mar

R EACHED BY A WINDING dirt track, Il Burchio (a *Club Ippico* - riding club)
is an informal, family-run country house in rustic style: white-washed
walls, terracotta floors, wrought iron bedsteads, wooden furniture and
plenty of pretty floral fabrics. Not surprisingly the emphasis is on riding,
with 20 or so horses and qualified instructors at the guests' disposal, but
for non-riders there's also a pool with hydro-massage, and golf and tennis
nearby. As well as supervised hacks, the club will organize mountain-bike
trails, and wine-tasting, gastronomic and art tours. Traditional Tuscan
meals are eaten at one table.

FATTORIA RIGNANA

COUNTRY GUESTHOUSE

*Rignana, Badia a Passignano,
Greve in Chianti, 50022 Firenze*

TEL (055) 852065
FAX (055) 8544874
E-MAIL rignana@tuscany.net
FOOD breakfast
PRICE € **CLOSED** Nov-Mar

O NCE AT THE LOVELY Badia a Passignano the fast road to Florence
becomes a long, unsurfaced one leading through unspoilt Chianti
countryside to this clutter of stone farmhouses and an 18thC villa, surrounded by vineyards, woodland and olive groves. (The farm, which dates
back to the 11th century when Rignana was a castle on the
Florence/Siena border, produces wine and oil.) The welcoming owners,
who offer bed and breakfast, are Cosimo Gericke and Sveva Rocco di
Torrepadula, and the accommodation, though simple, is not unstylish.
The villa has four double rooms, and the *fattoria* has seven. A lovely
swimming pool is set amongst the olive trees.

FIRENZE

RUFINA

FATTORIA DI PETROGNANO

FARM GUESTHOUSE

Via di Petrognano 40, Pomino,
Rufina, 50060 Firenze

TEL (055) 8318812/867
FAX (055) 242918
E-MAIL lagoria@dada.it
FOOD breakfast, lunch, dinner
PRICE € **CLOSED** Nov-Easter

MAGNIFICENTLY LOCATED high in the Rufina hills in the famous Pomino wine-making area, this is very much a place for those who like simple, unstuffy surroundings, a family atmosphere and fine views. The estate, with its 16thC manor house, belonged to the bishops of Fiesole until 1864 when it was sold to the Galeotti Ottieri della Ciaja family, who own it to this day. The charmingly furnished apartments are housed in restored farm buildings and meals are served in the converted stables at a long communal table beneath white arches. Local train to centre of Florence (20 minutes). Pool and tennis courts. [There are eight apartments.]

SAN CASCIANO

LA GINESTRA

FARMHOUSE APARTMENTS

Via Pergolato 3, San Pancrazio,
50020 Firenze

TEL & FAX (055) 8249245
E-MAIL laginestra@ftbcc.it
WEBSITE www.laginestra.org
FOOD lunch, dinner
PRICE €€
CLOSED never

TRUE 'AGRITURISMO': a working farm producing organic produce for its restaurant. Two isolated farmhouses are available, one divided into apartments (simple rustic style); the other takes groups of up to 13 people. Peace is assured - it's in the depths of Chianti country, surrounded by cypress and oak woods, and a long way even to the nearest bar. But you won't get bored: farm tours, cookery classes and mountain biking are all laid on, and the sights of Florence and Siena are within easy driving distance. Tuscan and Mediterranean dishes are the staples of its cosy restaurant in the original barn.

FIRENZE

VILLA LA MONTAGNOLA

COUNTRY VILLA

*Via della Montagnola 110/112,
Strada in Chianti, Firenze*

TEL (055) 858485
FAX (055) 8587003
E-MAIL none
FOOD breakfast
PRICE ⓔⓔ **CLOSED** never

A SOLID 19THC VILLA which fronts the busy SS222 Chiantigiano road, but benefits from lovely views from its rear. Recently fully renovated, it now has all the modern amenities and is more than comfortable, while still retaining the look and feel of a traditional, homely Tuscan villa. Bedrooms are large, airy and, like the rest of the hotel, well kept. Public rooms are filled with polished wood furniture and a mixed bag of paintings. There is an outdoor barbeque. We found the atmosphere somewhat soulless – no complaints, but no buzz.

PODERE SOVIGLIANO

COUNTRY GUESTHOUSE

*Via Magliano 9, Tavernelle Val
di Pesa, 50028 Firenze*

TEL (055) 8076217
FAX (055) 8050770
E-MAIL sovigliano@ftbcc.it
FOOD breakfast
PRICE ⓔⓔ **CLOSED** never

THERE IS A REASSURING AIR about these two solid, Tuscan farmhouse buildings with their massive walls and old-fashioned dovecot, set on a vineyard in hilly countryside behind Tavarnelle, with beautiful views of the Chianti landscape. The self-catering accommodation consists of three one-bedroom studio apartments and one two bedroom apartment, all with their own kitchens and living areas, plus four double rooms with shared kitchen and open fireplace. Simply but effectively furnished, with old wardrobes and wrought iron bedsteads, they have independent access to the garden. Swimming pool and mountain bikes. Chianti wine, olive oil and honey from the estate are for sale.

FIRENZE

LA VOLPAIA

FARM GUESTHOUSE

Strada di Vico 3-9, 50050 Vico d'Elsa, Firenze

TEL (055) 8073063
FAX (055) 8073170
E-MAIL none
WEBSITE www.lavolpaia.it
FOOD breakfast
PRICE €
CLOSED never

VAL D'ELSA IS BECOMING almost as popular with tourists as the main Chianti drag with easy access to Florence, Siena, Volterra and San Gimignano. This square 16thC villa and converted farmhouse with a small but spectacularly sited swimming pool offers a warm welcome and pleasantly decorated bedrooms.The sitting room has very much the feel of a private house, with interesting artefacts, harmonious use of fabrics and agreeable lighting. Riding. Half-board only.

GROSSETO

CINIGIANO

CASTELLO DI VICARELLO
~ RESTORED CASTLE ~

Via Vicarello 1, Cinigiano, 58044 Poggi del Sasso, Grosseto
TEL (0564) 990718 **FAX** (0564) 990718
E-MAIL info@vicarello.it **WEBSITE** www.vicarello.it

THE IMPOSING 12THC feudal castle of Vicarello stands proud on a rocky spur high above the rolling hinterland between the sea and Monte Amiata in the southern Maremma. Carlo Baccheschi bought it in the early 80s, but has only recently completed the restoration. His wife Aurora lived in Bali for many years and has filled the castle with her marvellous collection of antique Balinese furniture. They run their home like an exclusive, discreet yet relaxed, house party. Three of the enormous suites are housed in the castle itself, while two more are in the grounds (one in an ex-chapel). All have working fireplaces, tiny, ingeniously-hidden kitchen units, and are well-stocked with an eclectic collection of curios, arty books and magazines. The spectacular terraced grounds blend perfectly into the remote countryside; rosemary, lavender and sage border sloping lawns while olive and vines cover the hillside below. Two pools and plenty of hidden corners furnished with long chairs make it easy to relax in private. Aurora is a fabulous cook and bakes bread daily for breakfast which is served in an enormous country kitchen. She will also cook dinner on request. Carlo's fine wines and olive oil complement the abundant fresh produce grown in the vegetable garden.

~

NEARBY Grosseto (28km), Siena (40 kms).
LOCATION Off the SS 223, 15 kms south east of Paganico, just north of Cinigiano; car parking
FOOD breakfast; lunch and dinner on request
PRICE €€€€
ROOMS 6 suites, all with bath; all rooms have hairdrier
FACILITIES sitting room, breakfast room, 2 pools (one heated), garden, terraces
CREDIT CARDS AE, DC, MC, V **DISABLED** not suitable
PETS on request **CLOSED** never
PROPRIETORS Carlo and Aurora Baccheschi-Berti

Grosseto

Porto Ercole

Il Pellicano
~ Seaside Hotel ~

Cala dei Santi, 58018 Porto Ercole, Grosseto
Tel (0564) 858111 **Fax** (0564) 833418
E-MAIL Pr@Pellicanohotel.com **WEBSITE** www.Pellicanohotel.com

Porto Ercole is one of those fashionable little harbours where wealthy Romans moor their boats at weekends. Il Pellicano is an elegant, russet-coloured vine-clad villa with gardens tumbling down to the rocky shoreline, where the flat rocks have been designated the hotel's 'private beach'. It offers the luxury and exclusivity you might expect from a very expensive four-star seaside hotel but manages at the same time to preserve the style and informality of a private Tuscan villa – and the exposed beams, stone arches and antique features make it feel much older than it really is. Antique country-house furnishings are offset by whitewashed walls, brightly coloured stylish sofas and large vases of flowers. Fish and seafood are the best things in the restaurant – if you can stomach the prices. Meals in summer are served on the delightful open-air terrace in the garden, or beside the pool where the spread of antipasti is a feast for the eyes. Service is impeccable. Peaceful bedrooms, many in two-storey cottages, combine antiques and modern fabrics. The majority are cool and spacious, and all of them have a terrace or balcony. Watch out for swarms of mosquitoes, warns our inspector.

~

Nearby Orbetello (16 km).
Location 4 km from middle of resort; car parking
Food breakfast, lunch, dinner
Price €€€€€
Rooms 27 double; 14 suites (6 de luxe), all with bath and shower; all rooms have central heating, air conditioning, minibar, phone, cable TV
Facilities restaurants, bars, sitting area; terraces; beauty centre, heated sea water swimming pool; clay-pigeon shooting, tennis, riding, water-skiing
Credit cards AE, DC, MC, V
Disabled access difficult but some ground floor rooms
Pets not accepted **Closed** Nov-Mar
Languages English, French, Spanish, German **Proprietor** Mrs Roberto Scio

GROSSETO

MONTEMERANO

VILLA ACQUAVIVA
COUNTRY HOTEL

Acquaviva, Montemerano,
58050 Grosseto

TEL (0564) 602890
FAX (0564) 602895 **E-MAIL**
info@relaisvillaacquaviva.com
FOOD breakfast
PRICE €€
CLOSED never

DEEP IN THE HEART of the Maremma and close to the thermal springs and mud-baths of Saturnia, this pleasant family-run hotel, formerly a nobleman's villa, has been furnished with care and taste, using rustic antiques and bright fabrics. The garden, with its shady pines and terrace, is a major feature: it boasts a huge pool, and views to the nearby hilltop village of Montemerano. In fine weather you can of course eat a delicious home breakfast outside. The restaurant, La Limonaia di Villa Acquaviva, overlooking the pool, serves wines from the estate's own vineyard and fresh produce from the farm. There's a tennis court, and mountain bikes for hire. Guests get use of a privileged area of the Terme di Saturnia.

MONTIERI

RIFUGIO PRATEGIANO
MOUNTAIN HOTEL

Via Prategiano 45, Montieri,
58026 Grosseto

TEL (0566) 997703
FAX (0566) 997891
E-MAIL none
FOOD breakfast, lunch, dinner
PRICE €-€€
CLOSED Nov-Easter

A 'RIFUGIO' IS NORMALLY a mountain hostel with basic facilities for tired walkers. This hotel, though still simple, has more to offer: a swimming pool, restaurant, riding excursions, mountain biking, canoeing and tennis, as well as an attractive location high in the Maremma hills. Here the air is always fresh even during the hottest summers. Although the bedrooms are unexciting, there is a congenial bar, high-ceilinged sitting room and country-style restaurant with a warm tiled floor and fireplace, which specializes in hearty local food. The National Park of Maremma is close by.

GROSSETO

SATURNIA

VILLA CLODIA
COUNTRY VILLA

Via Italia 43, Saturnia, 58050 Grosseto

TEL (0564) 601212
FAX (0564) 601305
E-MAIL none
FOOD breakfast
PRICE €
CLOSED 9 Jan-Feb

A TURN-OF-THE-CENTURY VILLA on the outskirts of the medieval village of Saturnia, painted gleaming white and well maintained by owner Giancarlo Ghezzi, ingeniously constructed around a limestone escarpment that gives great character to the interiors. Some bedrooms have access to a terrace overlooking the valley, and all can enjoy the morning sun pouring in to the light, airy breakfast room. There's a swimming pool in the nicely kept garden. Nearby you have not only thermal springs, but an 18-hole golf course, the Forest of Tombolo di Feniglia and the Maremma National Park.

LIVORNO

BIBBONA

PODERE LE MEZZELUNE
∽ COUNTRY GUESTHOUSE ∽

Mezzelune 126, 57020 Bibbona, Livorno
TEL (0586) 670266 **FAX** (0586) 671814
E-MAIL relais@lemezzelune.it **WEBSITE** www.lemezzelune.it

LUISA CHIESA ALFIERI left her business in Parma and moved to Tuscany in the mid 90s when she and her late husband bought this stone farmhouse and its surrounding land. The property (which produces a fine olive oil) lies in the northern Maremma, between the coast and the hills just inland from the popular beach resort of Cecina, but is light years away from the seaside crowds: this is a place for those genuinely seeking peace and quiet. The house has been beautifully furnished using natural colours and plenty of wood. The ground floor is a sunny open-plan space with a vast fireplace, a big rustic breakfast table and sitting areas with shelves of books and magazines. It has a comfortable, lived-in feel; hats and jackets hang on the coat rack while inviting smells of baking emanate from the kitchen area. The four simple, sunny bedrooms have stripped beams, hardwood floors, old wrought iron beds and gleaming white bathrooms; each has a private terrace. Two self-catering apartments occupy converted outbuildings in the garden. There is no TV and no pool at Le Mezzelune, but you will not be bored if you enjoy walking, riding, cycling, wine and good food, all of which is on hand nearby.

∽

NEARBY beaches (7km), Cecina (10 km), Volterra (30 km).
LOCATION 10 km south east of Cecina, on road to Bibbona; in open countryside; ample car parking
FOOD breakfast
PRICE €€
ROOMS 4 doubles and 2 apartments sleeping 2-3; all rooms have shower, minibar, hairdrier
FACILITIES breakfast room, sitting room, terraces, garden, bikes on request
CREDIT CARDS AE, DC, MC, V
DISABLED no special facilities
PETS not accepted **CLOSED** never
PROPRIETOR Luisa Chiesa Alfieri

LUCCA

LOCANDA L'ELISA
~ COUNTRY VILLA ~

Via Nuova per Pisa (SS 12 bis), Massa Pisana, 55050 Lucca
TEL (0583) 379737 **FAX** (0583) 379019
E-MAIL info@locandalelisa.com **WEBSITE** www.locandalelisa.com

A FRENCH OFFICIAL OF THE NAPOLEONIC times who accompanied the Emperor's sister, Elisa Baciocchi, to Lucca acquired this 18thC villa for his own residence. Perhaps that accounts for the discernibly French style of the house that makes it unique among Tuscan hotels. A square building, three storeys high, painted in an arresting blue, with windows and cornices picked out in gleaming white, the villa stands just off the busy old Pisa-Lucca road.

The restorers have fortunately avoided the oppressive Empire style (which, in any case, the small rooms would not have borne) and aimed throughout at lightness and delicacy. The entrance is a symphony in wood, with geometrically patterned parquet flooring and panelled walls, and the illusion of space created with large mirrors. To the right is a small sitting room, furnished with fine antiques and Knole sofas. A round 19thC conservatory is now the romantic restaurant; the food is unpretentious and excellent, with an emphasis on fish. Each suite has been individually decorated using striped, floral and small-check patterns, canopied beds and yet more antiques – no expense has been spared. A glorious mature garden insulates it from the main road.

~

NEARBY Lucca (3 km); Pisa (15 km).
LOCATION 3 km S of Lucca on the old road to Pisa; car parking
FOOD breakfast, lunch, dinner
PRICE €€€€
ROOMS 1 double, 1 single, 8 suites, all with bath or shower; all rooms have phone, TV, air conditioning, minibar, safe, hairdrier
FACILITIES sitting rooms, restaurant, garden, swimming pool
CREDIT CARDS AE, DC, MC, V
DISABLED ground floor rooms available
PETS small dogs accepted
CLOSED early Jan- early Feb
MANAGER Leonardo Iurlo

LUCCA

ALBERGO PIETRASANTA
~ TOWN HOTEL ~

Via Garibaldi 35, 55045 Pietrasanta, Lucca
TEL (0584) 793726 **FAX** (0584) 793728 **E-MAIL** a.pietrasanta@versilia.toscana.it
WEBSITE www.albergopietrasanta.com

PIETRASANTA (THE 'SAINTED STONE') has long been associated with the marble industry. The world famous quarries at Carrara are nearby, and the attractive little town thrives on marble studios, bronze foundries and a subculture of artists from all over the world. Recently, tourism here has moved up-market, and the Pietrasanta is a response to this development. Opened in 1997, the hotel occupies elegant 17thC Palazzo Barsanti-Bonetti in the centre of town. The interior maintains many of the embellishments of a nobleman's house: intricate plasterwork, delicate frescoes, a couple of superbly carved marble fireplaces, spacious rooms and antiques. However, the addition of the owners' contemporary art collection adds a totally new dimension.

The comfortable, unfussy bedrooms have warm, parquet floors, armchairs, smart fabrics and varying colour schemes. Thoughtful extras (cool linen sheets, plenty of mirrors, well-designed lighting (and the tray of *vin santo* and biscuits) impressed our inspector. Downstairs, the winter garden doubles as a breakfast room and bar, while the pretty gravelled garden, dominated by three old palm trees, is a cool spot in summer.

~

NEARBY Pisa (25 km); Lucca (25 km); beaches (4 km).
LOCATION in town centre on pedestrian street; private garage
FOOD breakfast
PRICE €€€€
ROOMS 1 single, 8 double and twin, 10 suites, all with bath or shower; all rooms have phone, TV, minibar, air conditioning, safe
FACILITIES breakfast room/winter garden, gym, Turkish bath, garden, sitting rooms, bar **CREDIT CARDS** AE, DC, MC, V
DISABLED 2 adapted rooms **PETS** by arrangement **CLOSED** early Jan-Mar
LANGUAGES English, French, German
MANAGER Robert Esposito

LUCCA

SANTA MARIA DEL GIUDICE

VILLA RINASCIMENTO
~ COUNTRY VILLA ~

Santa Maria del Giudice, 55058 Lucca
TEL (0583) 378292 **Fax** (0583) 370238

ALMOST EXACTLY HALF-WAY between Pisa and Lucca, this hillside villa presents, at first sight, something of an architectural conundrum. On the right-hand side is a rosy coloured, rustic Renaissance villa, three storeys high, constructed with a mixture of brick and stone. Its main feature is a lovely corner loggia, enclosed by four brick arches supported by Doric columns in stone. On the left, it is joined by a much simpler farmhouse structure. The two are united by a long, paved terrace with lemon trees in large terracotta pots. One can breakfast here or take an *aperitivo* in the evening.

Inside, a more uniform rustic style prevails. The public rooms are all in a row, facing the terrace, and distinguished by having either exposed-beam or brick-vaulted ceilings, all immaculately restored and including interesting features such as the remnants of an old stone olive-press. Great effort has been put into the bedroom furnishings. Some of the bathrooms are small, but adequate.

Up the hill from the villa is the annex, with some more modern rooms and studios, and a pool designed to exploit to the full its hillside position.

~

NEARBY Lucca (9 km); Pisa (11 km).
LOCATION 9 km SW of Lucca in its own grounds; ample car parking
FOOD breakfast, dinner
PRICE €-€€
ROOMS 17 double, all with bath or shower, phone; some with TV; 4 simpler rooms and 6 studios (one-week rents from Saturdays) in annexe
FACILITIES sitting rooms, bar, restaurant, swimming pool
CREDIT CARDS MC, V
DISABLED one room with bathroom
PETS please check first **CLOSED** Nov to Mar; restaurant only, Wed
LANGUAGES English, German, French, Dutch
PROPRIETOR Carla Zaffora

LUCCA

ALLA CORTE DEGLI ANGELI
CASTLE HOTEL

Via degli Angeli 23, 55100 Lucca

TEL (0583) 469204
FAX (0583) 991989 **E-MAIL**
info@allacortedegliangeli.com
WEBSITE
www.allacortedegliangeli.com
FOOD breakfast
PRICE €€ **CLOSED** never

THE LOVELY WALLED TOWN of Lucca makes an excellent base for a few days: you can explore the town itself, visit nearby villas, drive up to the verdant Garfagnana or spend a day on the beach. This small, upmarket guesthouse is one of the few 'charming' places to stay within the walls. Downstairs, a reception area includes a small dining room (it must be said that we have had one negative comment about the breakfast) while on the upper floor, the six bedrooms (named after flowers) are elegantly and comfortably furnished and painted in pastel shades. Bathrooms all have Jacuzzi tubs.

PISA

MONTECATINI VAL DI CECINA

IL FRASSINELLO
~ FARMHOUSE ~

Montecatini Val di Cecina, 56040 Pisa
TEL (0588) 30080 **FAX** (0588) 30080
E-MAIL ilfrassinello@sirt.pisa.it **WEBSITE** www.ilfrassinello.com

THE DIFFICULT, UNSURFACED ROAD that brings you from Montecatini to Il Frassinello seems to last for ever and is certainly not for the weak-spirited. But it is also a guarantee of seclusion. You arrive at your destination to be greeted by the redoubtable Signora Schlubach, who decided to retire here and "not see too much action".

If ever a place has received the imprint of its owner, this is it. The spacious, pleasantly proportioned interiors are filled with the results of a lifetime's collecting on various continents: zebra rugs on the floors, the mounted heads of at least four different types of antelope, a bronze angel hovering over the kitchen door.

There are three rooms in the main villa, and four large self-contained apartments with new bathrooms in a separate building, each with a little kitchen and their own entrance and private terrace, where the minimum stay is three nights. It is possible to rent the whole house for twelve people on a weekly basis.

Guests are not expected to do very much: just relax, take a stroll down to the deer farm, or read a book. Breakfast is taken either in the homely kitchen, or outside under the wisteria-covered pergola.

~

NEARBY Volterra (23 km).
LOCATION 5 km from Montecatini Val di Cecina in middle of countryside, good walking in nearby woods
FOOD breakfast; dinner on request (sometimes)
PRICE rooms €; apartment €€€€ per week; discounts for longer stays. 35% to be payed on reservation
ROOMS 4 double all with bath or shower; 4 apartments
FACILITIES sitting room, garden, swimming pool, riding near by, ping-pong, petanque.
CREDIT CARDS not accepted **DISABLED** not suitable
PETS small dogs **CLOSED** Oct-Easter **LANGUAGES** English, French, German, Spanish
PROPRIETOR Elga Schlubach

PISA

PISA

ROYAL VICTORIA
~ TOWN HOTEL ~

Lungarno Pacinotti 12, 56126 Pisa
TEL (050) 940111 **FAX** (050) 940180
E-MAIL eds@royalvictoria.it **WEBSITE** www.royalvictoria.it

FAMOUS WORLDWIDE FOR ITS NOW not-so-leaning tower, Pisa has a long history as a tourist destination, having been an important stop on the Grand Tour. These days, its hotels are disappointingly short on charm with the exception of the Royal Victoria, a relic of that golden age of travel which occupies a *palazzo* on the north bank of the Arno. Its attraction lies in the rather funky retro atmosphere as opposed to its creatue comforts, but it has many fans and we are pleased to include it.

The hotel dates back some 160 years, although the *palazzo* itself is very much older. The old-fashioned lobby is adorned with potted palms and the walls are hung with framed letters from past guests who include Dickens, the Duke of Wellington and Ruskin. Upstairs, the bedrooms are fairly spartan with lumbering old furniture and 60s bathrooms (due to be renovated), but mattresses and fabrics are new. Room 202 is extraordinary, with creaky old parquet, floor-to-ceiling medieval-style *trompe l'oeil* frescoes and painted furniture. The breakfast room belongs to the same rather dreamy, bygone age. There are several sitting areas, but far the best place to relax with a book and an aperitif is the plant-filled roof terrace.

~

NEARBY Palazzo Reale; Piazza dei Cavalieri; Leaning Tower.
LOCATION on north bank of Arno with private garage and lift
FOOD breakfast
PRICES €€
ROOMS 48 doubles and twin, all but 8 with bath or shower; all rooms have phone, TV, hairdrier on request
FACILITIES sitting room, breakfast room, roof terrace
CREDIT CARDS AE, DC, MC, V
DISABLED no special facilities
PETS accepted
CLOSED never
PROPRIETORS Nicola and Maurizio Piegaja

PISA

PUGNANO

CASETTA DELLE SELVE
~ COUNTRY BED AND BREAKFAST ~

56010 Pugnano, Pisa
TEL & **FAX** (050) 850359 56010

YET ANOTHER ELEVATED Tuscan farmhouse, but this one has a personality all of its own thanks to the owner, Nicla Menchi, a most unusual host. The approach to the white building is through a thick chestnut wood. Once at the top of the rough 2-km drive, the peaceful surroundings, the flower-filled garden and the wonderful views from the red-tiled terrace start to work their magic.

The interiors are very different from the norm. For a start, Nicla's own vivid paintings occupy much of the wall space. The house is exceptionally well-maintained and the bedrooms have bold, bright colour schemes involving bedheads, rugs, bedspreads (all handmade by Nicla) and, of course, her pictures. It might be a little fussy for some tastes; even the coat hangers are colour co-ordinated. However, public areas are a little more restrained, but still full of pictures, books and ornaments. Breakfast (including fresh eggs, home-made cakes and jams) is, when possible, served on the terrace.

Nicla Menchi's enthusiasm for her home and her guests is infectious and many leave as her friend.

~

NEARBY Lucca (10km); Pisa (12 km); Beaches (15 km).
LOCATION In countryside 2 km off SS12, E of Pugnano, 10 km SW of Lucca; private car parking
FOOD breakfast
PRICE ⓔⓔ; minimum 3-day stay
ROOMS 6 doubles, all with bath or shower (two are adjacent)
FACILITIES garden, terrace, sitting room
CREDIT CARDS not accepted
DISABLED not suitable
PETS accepted **CLOSED** never
LANGUAGES French, a little English
PROPRIETOR Nicla Menchi

PISA

MONTOPOLI

QUATTRO GIGLI

TOWN HOTEL

*Piazza Michele da Monti 2,
Montopoli 56020, Pisa*

TEL (0571) 466878
FAX (0571) 466879
E-MAIL lodge@aolmaia.com
FOOD breakfast, lunch, dinner
PRICE € **CLOSED** 2 weeks Nov

THIS MODEST BUT PLEASANT inn stands in the central piazza of Montopoli, where it occupies a 14thC *palazzo* that was once the town's Podesta. It's been owned and run by the friendly Puccioni family since 1930 and, though better known as a restaurant than as a hotel, it nevertheless makes a more than adequate stopover, with the assurance of a good dinner before you retire to bed. Though the bedrooms are fairly standardized, some have balconies overlooking green valleys, while others look over the little town. The restaurant occupies the oldest part of the building and offers traditional local cuisine and a wide range of wines. In summer, dinner is served on a vine-shaded garden terrace by friendly staff. Pool.

RIGOLI

VILLA DI CORLIANO

COUNTRY VILLA

*Via Statale 50, Rigoli, San
Giuliano Terme, 56010 Pisa*

TEL (050) 818193
FAX (050) 818341
E-MAIL info@villacorliano.it
FOOD breakfast, lunch, dinner
PRICE €-€€ **CLOSED** never

USEFUL LOCATION for both Pisa and Lucca, and great value if the battered, aristocratic look is what you like. This 16thC baroque villa is the country home of a noble Italian family, opened as a hotel by the present owner, Count Ferdinando Agostini Venerosi della Seta, in 1980. Public rooms are decorated with frescoes depicting mythological scenes by the Florentine artist Andrea Boscoli, and are filled with chandeliers and statues. Bedrooms are large but vary in standard; not all have bathrooms. Friendly atmosphere. Famous Pisan chef, Sergio, has a restaurant in the grounds. One visitor was impressed; another found it marred by a lack of comforts.

PISA

VILLA RIODDI

COUNTRY HOTEL

Rioddi, Volterra, 56048 Pisa

TEL (0588) 88053
FAX (0588) 88074
E-MAIL info@hotelvillarioddi.it
WEBSITE www.hotelvillarioddi.it
FOOD breakfast
PRICE ⓔ
CLOSED 10 Jan-Mar

L ARGE OPEN SPACES spanned by stone arches and brick-vaulted ceilings characterize the ground floor of this 15thC villa just off the SS88 which leads south from Volterra in the direction of Cecina. The number of bedrooms has recently been increased from nine to 13: all are light, airy and fully equipped, though not exactly imaginative. There's a swimming pool in the garden, which has amazing 360-degree views, even by Tuscan standards. An apartment, sleeping two to four, is a recent addition, with its own private, sunny rooftop terrace.

PISTOIA

MASSA E COZZILE

VILLA PASQUINI
~ COUNTRY VILLA ~

Via Vacchereccia 56, Margine Coperta, Massa e Cozzile, 51010 Pistoia
TEL (0572) 72205 **FAX** (0572) 910888
E-MAIL info@villapasquini.com

STAY AT VILLA PASQUINI and you step back into the 19thC. Little has changed here, either in furnishings, or decoration, since then. Until five years ago, it was the autumn retreat of an aristocratic Roman family, the Pasquinis; then it was bought, fully furnished, by the present incumbents, who have lovingly preserved it, combining a family home with a most unusual hotel. Though it is something of a museum piece, the atmosphere is not stuffy. The family's enthusiasm is infectious, and the welcome is warm.

The bedrooms are, of course, all different, some quite grand (but not intimidating) with canopied beds. Bathrooms are old-fashioned, but well equipped. Many boast wonderful *trompe l`oeil* frescoes – lie in your tub contemplating a lakeland scene with swans and distant mountains.

In the attractive dining room – originally the entrance hall – the emphasis is on traditional recipes. Our reporter chose the fixed-price menu, was served five delicious courses and thought the price reasonable.

Outside, the gardens and terraces are lush with flowers.

~

NEARBY Montecatini Terme (8 km); Lucca (40 km); Pisa (60 km).
LOCATION off minor road 6 km N of Montecatini Terme in own grounds; ample car parking
FOOD breakfast, dinner
PRICE €
ROOMS 12 double, all with bath and shower, central heating
FACILITIES 2 sitting rooms, dining room, terraces, garden, walks
CREDIT CARDS AE, MC, V
DISABLED some suitable rooms
PETS not accepted
CLOSED 30 Nov-15 Mar
LANGUAGES English, German, French
PROPRIETORS Innocenti family

PISTOIA

MONTEVETTOLINI

VILLA LUCIA
~ FARMHOUSE BED AND BREAKFAST ~

Via dei Bronzoli 144, Montevettolini, 51010 Pistoia
TEL (0572) 617790 **FAX** (0572) 628817
E-MAIL lvallera@tin.it **WEBSITE** www.bboftuscany.com

LUCIA VALLERA also calls her delightful hillside farmhouse the 'B&B of Tuscany' and runs her establishment along English bed and breakfast lines – guests and family mingle informally, eating together in the traditional Tuscan kitchen or at the huge wooden table in the dining room if numbers require.

A strong Californian influence can be detected in the cooking and in the laid-back, elegant style of the place. (Lucia is an American of Italian extraction who has returned to Italy after living in the States.) There are plenty of up-to-date touches: CD player, satellite TV, computer. The clientèle, too, is mainly American – lawyers, doctors and so on – who are often on return visits.

The dining room has various dressers crammed with colourful china and glass; there is a double sitting room with comfortable sofas and armchairs in traditional fabrics, plus shelves of books. Bedrooms are attractive, with working fireplaces, patchwork bedspreads, terracotta floors and antique furniture. Bathrooms are decked in blue and white tiles, and are spotless. The house has a lovely garden, and looks up to the old town of Montevettolini.

~

NEARBY Montecatini Terme (5 km); Lucca (30 km); Pisa (50 km).
LOCATION on hillside outside Montevettolini; car parking
FOOD breakfast; dinner on request
PRICE €€€
ROOMS 5 double, 2 apartments for 2; all with bath and shower; all rooms have phone, TV, air conditioning
FACILITIES sitting room, conference room, terraces, garden, small pool
CREDIT CARDS not accepted
DISABLED no special facilities
PETS accepted **CLOSED** Nov-Apr **LANGUAGES** English, French, Spanish, German
PROPRIETOR Lucia Vallera

PISTOIA

PISTOIA

VILLA VANNINI
~ COUNTRY VILLA ~

Villa di Piteccio, 51030 Pistoia
TEL (0573) 42031 **FAX** (0573) 42551
E-MAIL info@volpe-uva.it **WEBSITE** www.volpe-uva.it

HERE IS A REAL GEM, well off the beaten track, and a complete contrast to the usual Tuscan villa. It has an Alpine feel: fir trees all around, low ceilings, green shutters, a little Swiss-style clock tower – and miles of marked footpaths all around, eventually leading up to the ski resort of Abetone. It is a haven for serious walkers.

The atmosphere at Villa Vannini is that of a private country house: there are no hotel signs. You will be greeted by an over-enthusiastic dog. An inviting smell of wood smoke pervades. The food served in the charming dining room or on the terrace under huge white umbrellas is carefully prepared and elegantly presented. Breakfasts are 'excellent' too, according to a recent reporter. Bedrooms are well above the standard for the price, beautifully and individually furnished, with polished parquet floors, oriental rugs, brass or wood bedsteads and lovely antique furniture and mirrors. Although Signora Vannini is about the place less than she was – she now has help from a delightful couple, the Bordonaros, whose cooking is 'inspirational and exquisitely fresh' – you'll still get a warm welcome. We've had an exceptional number of warmly approving readers' letters about the place.

~

NEARBY Pistoia (6 km); Florence (35 km); Lucca (45 km); Pistoiese hills.
LOCATION 6 km N of Pistoia, take Abetone road from Pistoia and branch right, the hotel is 2 km above Piteccio; car parking
FOOD breakfast, lunch, dinner
PRICE (€)
ROOMS 8 double and twin with bath (not all baths en suite)
FACILITIES 2 sitting rooms, games room, dining room, terrace, garden
CREDIT CARDS AE, DC, MC, V **DISABLED** no special facilities
PETS not accepted **CLOSED** never
LANGUAGES English, German, French
MANAGERS the Bordonaro family

PISTOIA

PESCIA

MARZALLA
AGITURISMO APARTMENTS

*Via Collecchio 1, Pescia, 51017
Pistoia*

TEL(0572) 490751
FAX (0572) 478332
E-MAIL info@marzalla.it
WEBSITE www.marzalla.it
FOOD none
PRICE €€€€
CLOSED never

THIS FAMILY-RUN Agriturismo has a pleasant setting on a 30-acre wine estate, overlooking the rolling Pistoiese hills. At its centre is a handsome old villa where the owners live; the seven apartments are in converted farmhouses. These are simply but tastefully decorated in a rustic style well suited to the exposed beams and terracotta-tiled floors; three have fireplaces and all have small private gardens and offer value for money. Three double bedrooms are also available, though not in high season. A separate restaurant, 'La Locanda', provides wholesome Tuscan food. There's a pool, table tennis and fishing lake, tennis courts and riding.

PRATO

BACCHERETO

FATTORIA DI BACCHERETO
~ COUNTRY GUESTHOUSE ~

Bacchereto, Via Fontemorana 179, 59015 Prato
TEL (055) 8717191 **FAX** (055) 8717191
E-MAIL fattoriadibacchereto@libero.it **WEBSITE** www.tuscany.net/bacchereto

ONE OF THE MOST ATTRACTIVE aspects of Fattoria di Bacchereto is its location high in the steep foothills of the Appenines, part of the famous Carmignano wine-growing district (which produces Italy's oldest recognized wine). Entirely isolated, with panoramic views, this little-frequented part of Tuscany is perfect for those who like to combine some city tourism (Florence, Pistoia, Lucca and Pisa are all within driving distance) with country walks and rural peace.

But do not expect luxury: the Fattoria is a working farm and the accommodation is relatively simple. The bedrooms and apartments are spread across the main villa, a rambling 18thC building with terraces and an arched loggia, and simpler farmhouses nearby. The rooms are furnished with time-worn rustic antiques, some in need of restoration, in a setting of terracotta floors and exposed-beam ceilings. The bathrooms are basic but functional.

Outside the villa are pergolas and an ornamental garden with a pond and a fountain, and slightly down the hillside is a small swimming pool. Breakfast is eaten at a long table near the kitchen; for other meals there is the excellent family restaurant nearby.
~

NEARBY Florence (25 km); Pistoia (18 km).
LOCATION 20 km W of Florence, near Carmignano, in own grounds; car parking
FOOD breakfast
PRICE €
ROOMS 7 double, some with private bathrooms; 4 apartments for 4 to 8 people
FACILITIES breakfast room, sitting room, gardens, swimming pool; family restaurant nearby
CREDIT CARDS accepted **DISABLED** not suitable
PETS on request **CLOSED** never
LANGUAGES English, French
PROPRIETOR Rossella Bencini Tesi

PRATO

VILLA RUCELLAI
~ COUNTRY VILLA ~

Via di Canneto 16, 59100 Prato
TEL & FAX (0574) 460392
E-MAIL canneto@masternet.it **WEBSITE** www.villarucellai.it

INDUSTRIAL PRATO creeps almost to the door of this mellow old villa, and a railway line skirts the property, but this should not deter you from staying in this special place. The views from the loggia and lovely terrace – filled with lemon trees – are unsightly, but are more than compensated for by the cultured atmosphere of the house, the warm welcome and the modest prices. Behind the estate rise the beautiful Pratese hills, which can be explored on foot.

The origins of the Villa Rucellai date back to a medieval watchtower, and it has been in the venerable Rucellai family since 1759. Guests have the run of the main part of the house, with its baronial hall and comfortable, lived-in sitting room, filled with pictures and books. Breakfast is self-service and eaten around a communal table in the homely dining room. Bedrooms are simply furnished and full of character, reflecting what a recent visitor confirmed is the main and rare attribute of the place - that it gives no hint of being anything other than a cultivated family house. A recent visitor was impressed overall, but had reservations about the homemade food and wine. There are two excellent restaurants nearby - La Fontana and Logli Mario - and directions to the former help with finding the Villa.

~

NEARBY Prato; Florence (20 km).
LOCATION in narrow street in Bisenzio river valley, 4 km NE of Prato, (keep parallel with river and train tracks on your left); car parking and grounds
FOOD breakfast
PRICE €
ROOMS 10 double, one family room; all have bath or shower; central heating
FACILITIES dining room, sitting room, TV room, terrace, pool
CREDIT CARDS V, MC, DC **DISABLED** not suitable **PETS** not usually accepted
CLOSED never **LANGUAGES** English, French
PROPRIETORS Rucellai Piqué family

SIENA

CASTELLINA IN CHIANTI

BELVEDERE DI SAN LEONINO
~ COUNTRY HOTEL ~

S. Leonino, Castellina in Chianti, 53011 Siena
TEL (0577) 740887 **FAX** (0577) 740924
E-MAIL info@hotelsanleonino.com **WEBSITE** www.hotelsanleonino.com

TOURISM HAS BEEN booming in Chianti over the past few years, especially in the commune of Castellina. It is easy to see why: rolling countryside liberally sprinkled with villas, the great art cities within driving distance and a surplus of farmhouses left by people migrating to the cities.

San Leonino is a typical case: a squat, square 15thC house with its barn and stables, built from the light-coloured local stone. The farmyard has been turned into a garden. A tree-shaded terrace has been created at the back, right at the edge of the vineyards, and tucked away out of sight is the swimming-pool. The restoration of the interiors has been meticulously done so that it is difficult to believe that the house is more than five hundred years old.

Sitting areas have been created out of the stables: wide, open rooms spanned by crescent-shaped brick arches. If we have one complaint, it is that the furnishing here would be more suitable for an airport lounge than a Tuscan farmhouse: the long, anonymous modern couches clash badly with the rustic ambience. Bedrooms are of a much higher standard. Prices are good value for this area.

~

NEARBY Siena (15 km); San Gimignano (30 km); Florence (50 km).
LOCATION 15 km N of Siena, in its own grounds; car parking
FOOD breakfast, dinner, lunch on request
PRICE €€
ROOMS 28 double, all with bath or shower, phone, hairdrier
FACILITIES sitting room, restaurant, bar, terrace, gardens, swimming pool, internet
CREDIT CARDS AE, MC, V
DISABLED not suitable
PETS not accepted **CLOSED** mid Nov-mid Mar
LANGUAGES English, French, German
PROPRIETOR Marco Orlandi

SIENA

CASTELLINA IN CHIANTI

IL COLOMBAIO
~ COUNTRY HOTEL ~

Via Chiantigiana 29, Castellina in Chianti, 53011 Siena
TEL (0577) 740444 **FAX** (0577) 740402
E-MAIL info@albergoilcolombaio.it **WEBSITE** www.albergoilcolombaio.it

A NEW ADDITION to the typically Tuscan farmhouse hotels that cluster around Castellina in Chianti, Il Colombaio is a successful example of a proven formula, and prices are still very reasonable. As you come from Greve in Chianti on the busy Chiantigiana road (SS 222), you will notice Il Colombaio on the right, surrounded by lawns, shrubs and trees. Stone built and capped with the tiled roofs at odd angles to one another so characteristic of Tuscany, the house has a pleasing aspect. It is, however, close to the road.

The restoration has been carried out with attention to detail, using country furniture to complement the rustic style of the building. The sitting room, which used to be the farm kitchen, is spacious and light with beamed ceilings, a traditional open fireplace and, in the corner, the old stone sink now filled with house plants. Breakfast is served in a small stone-vaulted room on the terrace.

Fifteen of the bedrooms are in the main house (the other six are in an annex across the road). All have been furnished with wrought iron beds and old-fashioned dressing tables, and all have modern bathrooms.

The lack of a restaurant is not a problem as there are plenty of good eateries nearby.

~

NEARBY Siena (20 km); Florence (40 km); San Gimignano (30 km).
LOCATION just N of Castellina in Chianti; car parking
PRICE €
ROOMS 15 double with bath or shower; all rooms have phone, TV, hairdrier
FACILITIES sitting room, breakfast room, garden, swimming pool
CREDIT CARDS AE, DC, MC V
DISABLED access possible
PETS not accepted **CLOSED** never
LANGUAGES English, French, German
MANAGER Roberta Baldini

SIENA

CASTELLINA IN CHIANTI

PALAZZO SQUARCIALUPI
~ TOWN HOTEL ~

Via Ferruccio, 26 Castellina in Chianti 53011 Siena
TEL (0577) 741186 **FAX** (0577) 740386
E-MAIL squarcialupi@tuscany.net **WEBSITE** www.tuscany.net/squarcia

PALAZZO SQUARCIALUPI is set right in the heart of the Medieval village of Castellina in Chianti, and when our reporter first visited, she was struck by the friendly, peaceful atmosphere and the lovely rooms.

It is a 14thC stone building with arched doors and windows, which was formerly an imposing farm residence. It has been renovated in a simple, stylish way, while retaining its traditional farm character. There are seventeen large bedrooms and suites with plain white walls, beamed ceilings and dark wooden furniture; downstairs is a rustic sitting room in muted tones of white, cream and terracotta, and another elegant room with frescoes.

Palazzo Squarcialupi is bound to delight those with an interest in sampling the local wine. Chianti Classico continues to be produced in the Fattoria, and barrels of 'La Castellina', the house wine, line the stone-vaulted cellar. Guests can taste the vintages in the bar or in the wine-tasting room, or on the terrace while admiring magnificent views of the Chianti countryside.

~

NEARBY Siena (18 km); Florence (40 km); San Gimignano (30 km).
LOCATION in town centre, overlooking valley
FOOD buffet breakfast; light meals in the bar
PRICE €€€–€€€€
ROOMS 9 double; 8 suites; all with bath or shower; all rooms have phone, TV, mini-bar, central heating, air conditioning
FACILITIES breakfast room, 2 sitting rooms, bar, terrace, garden, pool, wine cellar
CREDIT CARDS MC, V
DISABLED 2 suitable rooms
PETS small pets accepted
CLOSED mid-Jan-mid-Mar
LANGUAGES English, French, German, Spanish
PROPRIETORS Targioni family

SIENA

LE PIAZZE
~ COUNTRY HOTEL ~

Le Piazze, Castellina in Chianti, 53011 Siena
TEL (0577) 743190 **FAX** (0577) 743191
E-MAIL lepiazze@chiantinet.it **WEBSITE** www.locandalepiazze.it

A WELCOME ADDITION to the booming hotel scene in the area around Castellina in Chianti which, we feel, has the edge on many of its competitors. Although only 6 km from the bustling town, the hotel is in completely secluded countryside reached by a long unsurfaced road which seems to go on forever.

The hotel is, needless to say, a converted 17thC farmhouse, but in this case the owners have deployed more imagination and a greater sense of elegance than usual. The buffet breakfast, for instance, is served on tiled sideboards in a room adjacent to the kitchen and separated from it by a glass partition. Or you can remove yourself to any of the numerous terraces that surround the house for uninterrupted views of classical Chianti countryside.

Rustic antiques have, of course, been used in the furnishing with the usual terracotta, exposed beams and white plaster, but here and there the pattern is broken by pieces from Indonesia. Bedrooms are individually furnished with lavish use of striped fabrics (avoid those in the roof space – they can become unbearably hot) and bathrooms are large, with Jacuzzis or walk in showers big enough for a party.

~

NEARBY Siena (27 km); Florence (50 km).
LOCATION 6 km W of Castellina in Chianti; car parking
FOOD breakfast; lunch and dinner on request
PRICE €€€
ROOMS 20 double and twin with bath or shower; all rooms have phone
FACILITIES sitting room, breakfast room, bar, terraces, garden, swimming pool
CREDIT CARDS AE, DC, MC, V
DISABLED one specially adapted room
PETS quiet dogs accepted by arrangement **CLOSED** Nov-April
LANGUAGES English, French, German
PROPRIETOR Maureen Skelly Bonini

SIENA

CASTELLINA IN CHIANTI

SALIVOLPI
~ COUNTRY GUESTHOUSE ~

Via Fiorentina, Castellina in Chianti, 53011 Siena
TEL (0577) 740484 **FAX** (0577) 740998
E-MAIL info@hotelsalivolpi.com **WEBSITE** www.hotelsalivolpi.com

W E REMAIN PLEASANTLY SURPRISED by the excellent value offered by the Salivolpi in this popular part of Chianti. Prices for a double have not increased significantly, a sure sign of high advance bookings and a satisfied clientèle that returns year after year. Not that this country guesthouse in any way resembles a cheap alternative. Of the many converted farmhouses in the area, Salivolpi has the edge not just in terms of price but also because of its pleasant grounds and its swimming pool.

The buildings consist of the low stone farmhouses typical of Chianti, surrounded by lawns dotted with flower beds and terracotta urns. The thick walls and stone windows are designed to keep out the intense summer sun and an astute use of space and simple, white walls prevents any sensation of gloominess.

Most of the furniture in the common areas and bedrooms is rustic antique with a few non-intrusive modern pieces; those in the older building are more characteristic. The whole place is watched over by a professional and attentive staff. Breakfast is the only meal served but there is no shortage of good restaurants in the vicinity.

~

NEARBY Siena (21 km); San Gimignano (31 km); Florence (45 km).
LOCATION 500m outside town, on road to San Donato in Poggio; car parking
FOOD breakfast
PRICE €
ROOMS 19 double and twin, all with bath or shower; all rooms have phone
FACILITIES sitting room, breakfast room, garden, swimming pool
CREDIT CARDS MC, V
DISABLED no special facilities
PETS not accepted **CLOSED** never
LANGUAGES English, German, French
PROPRIETOR Angela Orlandi

SIENA

CASTELLINA IN CHIANTI

TENUTA DI RICAVO
↜ COUNTRY HOTEL ↜

Ricavo 4, Castellina in Chianti, 53011 Siena
TEL (0577) 740221 **FAX** (0577) 741014
E-MAIL ricavo@ricavo.com **WEBSITE** www.ricavo.com

LIKE TUSCAN COOKING, the secret of Tenuta di Ricavo's success is easy to describe but difficult to reproduce: simple local ingredients of the highest quality, artfully combined. Here at Ricavo, all the essential elements are present: a hamlet of small stone houses strung out along a hillside, attentive Swiss-Italian owners, and the well tried formula of a country hotel in the heart of Chianti. The centre of the hamlet is a gravel piazza divided along the diagonal by a row of cypresses. On one side is the main house which now contains the restaurant, sitting rooms and some of the bedrooms. On the other side of the cypresses are the former farm buildings and peasant dwellings. The hamlet stretches back some distance, so there is no danger of guests crowding in on one another.

Furnishings and decoration are of the highest standards. Bedrooms in the main house are more spacious and formal; the others have more individual character, and many have terraces looking on to the wooded valley. The bathrooms have all been recently re-done, and there is a new swimming pool. One of the finest hotels in the Chianti region – and with a top-class restaurant too.

↜

NEARBY Siena (22 km); Florence (45 km).
LOCATION 4 km N of Castellina in Chianti; car parking
FOOD breakfast, lunch (in summer), dinner
PRICE €€€ 3-day minimum stay in high season
ROOMS 13 double and twin, 2 single, 8 suites, all with bath or shower; all rooms have phone, TV, safe, minibar
FACILITIES sitting rooms, bar, restaurant, terrace, 2 swimming pools, table tennis
CREDIT CARDS MC, V **DISABLED** ground floor rooms available
PETS not accepted **CLOSED** Nov-Easter; restaurant closed Sun
LANGUAGES English, French, German
PROPRIETOR Christina Lobrano-Scotoni and Alessandro Lobrano

SIENA

CASTELNUOVO BERARDENGA

RELAIS BORGO SAN FELICE
~ HILLTOP VILLAGE ~

Borgo San Felice, Castelnuovo Berardenga, 53019 Siena
TEL (0577) 359260/396561 **FAX** (0577) 359089
E-MAIL info@borgosanfelice.it **WEBSITE** www.borgosanfelice.com

LARGER THAN MOST of the entries in the guide, Borgo San Felice can legitimately be included because this carefully renovated hilltop hamlet is like a collection of charming small hotels. Surrounded by cypresses and the vineyards of the renowned San Felice estate, the tranquil village has the air of being suspended in time. No intrusive neon signs, no lines of cars, just the original Tuscan qualities of perfectly proportioned space setting off simple buildings of brick and stone and topped by a jumble of terracotta roofs. Even the swimming pool (which can often resemble a gaping, blue gunshot wound) has been discreetly tucked away. Gravel paths, carved well-heads, pergolas, lemon trees in gigantic terracotta pots, a church, a bell tower and a chapel – one is in the presence of the essence of Tuscany.

All the original features of the various buildings have been retained: vaulted brick ceilings, imposing fireplaces, old tiled floors. The furniture is a stylish mixture of old and modern, and the sitting rooms are full of intimate alcoves. An elegant restaurant completes the picture. Top of the range – and so are the prices.

~

NEARBY Siena (17 km).
LOCATION 17 km NE of Siena in former estate village; car parking
FOOD breakfast, lunch, dinner
PRICE €€€€
ROOMS 15 suites, 24 double and twin, 4 single; all with bath or shower, phone, TV, minibar, air conditioning, hairdrier, safe
FACILITIES swimming pool, tennis courts, bowls court, billiards room, conference rooms, sitting rooms, beauty centre, gym, putting and pitching green
CREDIT CARDS AE, DC, MC, V
DISABLED access difficult
PETS not accepted **CLOSED** Nov-April
LANGUAGES English, French, Spanish and German
MANAGER Birgit Fleig

SIENA

CASTELNUOVO BERARDENGA

VILLA CURINA
~ COUNTRY VILLA ~

Curina, Castelnuovo Berardenga, 53019 Siena
TEL (0577) 355586**FAX** (0577) 355412
E-MAIL www.villacurina.it **WEBSITE** info@villacurina.it

A VIVACIOUS, convivial atmosphere pervades this hotel-and-apartment complex set in low, rolling countryside north of Siena; when we visited, it was full of activity with people enjoying themselves in the pool, playing tennis or going out for bike rides. In fact, some may find it too energetic for their requirements.

The main villa, surrounded by ornamental gardens and trees, is a large, cream-coloured, 18thC building and contains the bedrooms for guests as well as the principal public rooms. Most of the apartments are in three old stone farmhouses with small, brown-shuttered windows and connected by pathways of Siena brick.

The bedrooms are furnished in a slightly heavier version of the standard rustic manner, but they are all comfortable and well-lit. An attractive restaurant, spanned by strong brick arches, serves fresh produce from the estate along with its own wine and grappa.

Terraced gardens covered with a profusion of flowers and geometric box-hedges lead down from the side of the villa to the swimming-pool and its large, terracotta-paved solarium. A quieter, shadier gravel terrace can be found at the back.

~

NEARBY Castelnuovo Berardenga (6 km); Siena (20 km).
LOCATION 6 km W of Castelnuovo Berardenga in its own grounds; ample car parking
FOOD breakfast, dinner
PRICE €-€€
ROOMS 15 doubles, all with bath or shower, phone, TV; 12 apartments for 2-6 persons
FACILITIES restaurant, terrace, gardens, bikes, swimming pool, tennis
CREDIT CARDS MC,V **DISABLED** no special facilities
PETS not accepted **CLOSED** Nov-Mar/Apr **LANGUAGES** English, German, French
MANAGER Franco Sbardelati

SIENA

CETONA

LA FRATERIA
~ FORMER CONVENT ~

Convento di San Francesco, Cetona, 53040 Siena
TEL (0578) 238015 **FAX** (0578) 239220
E-MAIL frateria@fbcc.it **WEBSITE** www.mondox.it

ONE OF THE MORE UNUSUAL entries in this guide and not a hotel in the strict sense but a place of hospitality run by a community that has withdrawn from the world. The buildings, grouped around a hillside church founded in 1212 by St. Francis, are constructed out of light, golden stone, and form a rambling complex. Only seven rooms and suites are available, so, even when it is fully booked one never has the sensation of being in a busy hotel but a place of retreat. There is no swimming pool and none of the rooms have a television.

This may sound monastic, but the setting and furnishings are of the same standard as a top-class hotel: antiques, paintings and colourful wooden carvings (generally religious in theme) and spacious rooms with stone and beige stucco walls. The restaurant is unexpectedly sophisticated (and expensive), serving a mixture of refined and hearty food using fresh produce from the gardens.

A stroll around the monastery with its church and chapel, cloisters and courtyards, and hushed, tranquil air will help you realize why the young people of this community want to share their peace.
~

NEARBY Pienza (40 km); Montepulciano (26 km); Montalcino (64 km); Siena (89 km).
LOCATION 26 km S of Montepulciano; car parking
FOOD breakfast, lunch, dinner
PRICE €€€
ROOMS 5 double, 2 suites, all with bath or shower; all rooms have phone, air conditioning, minibar, hairdrier
FACILITIES sitting rooms, restaurant, terrace, garden
CREDIT CARDS AE, MC, V
DISABLED no special facilities
PETS not accepted **CLOSED** Jan; restaurant Tues in winter **LANGUAGES** English
MANAGER Maria Grazia Daolio

SIENA

CHIANCIANO TERME

LA FOCE
~ COUNTRY APARTMENTS ~

Strada della Vittoria 63, 53042 Chianciano Terme, Siena
TEL AND FAX (0578) 69101
E-MAIL info@lafoce.com **WEBSITE** www.lafoce.com

ANYONE WHO IS FAMILIAR with the writing of Iris Origo will be particularly interested in La Foce, the estate whose history during the Second World War is so vividly described in her book, *War in the Val d'Orcia*. Iris died in 1988, but her family still live on the property in this remote but strangely beautiful corner of Tuscany, and they run it as a working farm.

Several of the buildings on the large estate have been converted into superior self-catering accommodation, ranging from the delightful two-person Bersagliere to the superb and quite grand Montauto which sleeps ten. The latter stands in its own extensive garden with lavender borders and a small pool.

Furnishings throughout the comfortable apartments are in sophisticated and tasteful country style, predominantly antique, but with a few well-chosen modern pieces. There is plenty of colour, provided by bright rugs, cushions and cheerful fabrics. Each has its own piece of private garden and the use of a pool. Music lovers will appreciate the excellent chamber music festival which takes place on the estate each July.

~

NEARBY Pienza (20 km); Montepulciano (10 km).
LOCATION 5 km SW of Chianciano Terme (follow the signs for Monte Amiata and Cassia); car parking
FOOD dinner on request
PRICE appartment sleeping 2 people €, weekly rates from £700; minimum rent 1 week
ROOMS 9 self-catering apartments/houses sleeping 2-14, all with bath and shower; all apartments/houses have phone, TV on request, central heating
FACILITIES swimming pools, tennis, playground, terraces, garden
CREDIT CARDS MC, V
DISABLED 2 specially adapted rooms
PETS not accepted **CLOSED** never
LANGUAGES English, French, German
PROPRIETORS Benedetta and Donata Origo

SIENA

GAIOLE IN CHIANTI

BADIA A COLTIBUONO
~ CONVERTED MONASTERY ~

Badia a Coltibuono, 53013 Gaiole in Chianti, Siena
TEL (0577) 74481 **FAX** (0577) 749235
E-MAIL badia@coltibuono.com **WEBSITE** www.coltibuono.com

SITUATED IN SPLENDID isolation on a hill in the heart of the Chianti winelands, the abbey of Badia a Coltibuono was founded in 1041 by Benedictine monks. Ancestors of the present owners acquired the property in the mid 1800s. Today, their descendants still live here and run a successful wine and olive oil business, a cooking school, a restaurant and the recently-opened accommodation.

The spacious guest bedrooms are housed in the ex-monks' cells in a wing of what was once the cloister. All have wonderful views. Beautifully furnished with family antiques (one has a fabulous set of Biedermeyer) and pictures, and with pretty country fabrics, they are homely rather than grand. Well-thumbed books fill bookshelves and the quaint bathrooms have old-fashioned tiles and quirky fittings. What it lacks in services is made up for by the atmosphere.

Guests can use the old library for peaceful reading while downstairs is a big living room where a fire burns in the huge grate on chilly evenings. Breakfast is served in an elegant dining room with French doors that open out on to a beautiful Italianate garden where the monks used to grow medicinal herbs. The restaurant offers elegant Tuscan cuisine with a twist.

~

NEARBY Chianti vineyards; Siena (35km); Radda (7km).
LOCATION near the junction of the SS408 and the SS429, 7 km east of Radda in Chianti; ample car parking
FOOD breakfast; lunch and dinner in adjoining restaurant
PRICE €€
ROOMS 8 double and twin, 2 singles, all with bath or shower; all rooms have hairdrier
FACILITIES breakfast room, sitting room, restaurant, terrace, garden, swimming pool, Turkish bath
CREDIT CARDS MC, V **DISABLED** not suitable
PETS accepted but please advise when booking **CLOSED** mid Dec-early Feb
PROPRIETORS Stucchi-Prinetti family

SIENA

GAIOLE IN CHIANTI

SAN SANO
~ COUNTRY VILLAGE HOTEL ~

San Sano, Gaiole in Chianti, 53010 Siena
TEL (0577) 746130 **FAX** (0577) 746156
E-MAIL info@sansanohotel.it **WEBSITE** www.sansanohotel.it

THE MEDIEVAL HAMLET of San Sano, a clutter of stone houses with uneven terracotta roofs, has at its heart an ancient defence tower, destroyed and rebuilt many times. Now, in its latest incarnation, this imposing structure forms the core of a delightful, family-run hotel in a relatively little visited, authentic part of Chianti.

The various buildings surrounding the tower (which houses some of the bedrooms; others have direct access to the grounds) give the hotel a rambling character, connected by narrow passageways, steep stairways and unexpected courtyards. The restoration has been meticulous and restrained. The decoration is in classic, rustic Tuscan style but with individual touches: carefully chosen antiques, colourful pottery and plenty of flowers. The dining room, in the former stables, spanned by a massive stone arch and still with the feeding trough, is a cool haven from the summer sun. Each bedroom has its individual character (one with nesting birds in its perforated walls, now glassed off) and gleaming, almost surgical bathrooms. Outside is a stone-paved garden at the foot of the tower and, at a slight remove, a hillside swimming pool.

~

NEARBY Radda in Chianti (9 km); Siena (25 km); Florence (60 km).
LOCATION hilltop hamlet in open countryside; car parking
FOOD breakfast, dinner
PRICE €€
ROOMS 12 double and twin, 2 single, all with shower, 2 with bath; all rooms have phone, TV, air conditioning, minibar, hairdrier
FACILITIES sitting areas, breakfast and dining room, garden, swimming pool
CREDIT CARDS AE, DC, MC, V
DISABLED 2 adapted rooms
PETS accepted **CLOSED** mid Nov-mid Mar
LANGUAGES English, German, French, Spanish
PROPRIETOR Marco Amabili

SIENA

MONTERIGGIONI

MONTERIGGIONI
∽ VILLAGE HOTEL ∽

Via 1 Maggio 4, Monteriggioni, 53035 Siena
TEL (0577) 305009/305010 FAX (0577) 305011
E-MAIL info@hotelmonteriggioni.net WEBSITE www.hotelmonteriggioni.net

VISITORS TO TUSCANY have been increasingly keen to drop by well-preserved, medieval Monteriggioni and spend a couple of hours relaxing in
the *piazza* (where a bar serves snacks), browsing the antique shops or
sampling the menu of Il Pozzo, one of the finest restaurants in the Siena
area. Finally, somebody had the bright idea that a small hotel would not go
amiss, especially since the town is peaceful and well placed for exploring
the locality.

A couple of old stone houses were knocked together and converted with
sure-handed lightness of touch to make this attractive hotel. The former
stables now make a large, light and airy public area used as a reception,
sitting room and breakfast room.

At the back, a door leads out to a well-tended garden running down to
the town walls, containing what is posibly the smallest swimming pool in
Tuscany. The bedrooms are perfectly acceptable, furnished to a high rus-
tic-antique standard with stylish hyper modern bathrooms.

∽

NEARBY Siena (10 km); San Gimignano (18 km); Florence (55 km); Volterra (40
km).
LOCATION within the walls of Monteriggioni, 10 km N of Siena; car parking nearby
FOOD breakfast
PRICE €€€
ROOMS 2 single, 10 double, all with shower; all rooms have phone, TV, minibar, air
conditioning, safe
FACILITIES sitting area, breakfast room, bar, garden, small swimming pool
CREDIT CARDS AE, DC, MC, V
DISABLED no special facilities
PETS not accepted CLOSED Jan-Feb
LANGUAGES English, French,German
MANAGER Michela Gozzi

SIENA

MONTERIGGIONI

SAN LUIGI
~ COUNTRY HOTEL ~

Strove, Via della Cerreta 38, Monteriggioni, 53030 Siena
TEL (0577) 301055 **FAX** (0577) 301167
E-MAIL info@relais-borgosanluigi.it **WEBSITE** www.borgosanluigi.it

THERE HAS BEEN NO SKIMPING or cutting corners in the conversion of the farm buildings of San Luigi to a country hotel with a difference, which we think will appeal to some readers, especially those travelling with a young family. A long, unpaved drive takes you through acres of grounds to the main building and reception. When we remarked on how green everything was, even in summer, we learned that this was originally an Etruscan settlement and that they always chose areas with supplies of underground water.

Certainly, the present owners of San Luigi have exploited the lush setting. The park is crammed with things to do: swimming, tennis, volleyball, basketball, bowls, even a giant chessboard. If lively group activity is not for you, there are acres of countryside for rambles and secluded corners to retreat to with a book.

It would be unfair to describe San Luigi as a holiday camp, but it would be equally misleading to recommend it to readers in search of a tranquil break. Guests, when we visited, seemed incredibly active – especially the younger ones – and copious buffet meals helped to fuel their energies.

~

NEARBY Monteriggioni (5 km); Siena (12 km); Florence (50 km).
LOCATION 5 km NW of Monteriggioni in its own spacious park; ample car parking
FOOD breakfast, lunch, dinner
PRICE €€€
ROOMS 2 single, 32 double, 5 apartments for 2-6 people, all with bath or shower
FACILITIES sitting room, restaurant, bar, gardens, tennis, volley and basketball, 2 swimming pools, giant chess
CREDIT CARDS AE, DC, MC, V **DISABLED** 2 rooms specially fitted
PETS small dogs accepted **CLOSED** never
LANGUAGES English, French, German, Spanish
PROPRIETOR Sig. Michelagnoli

SIENA

MONTICHIELLO DI PIENZA

L'OLMO
~ COUNTRY GUESTHOUSE ~

53020 Montichiello di Pienza, Siena
TEL (0578) 755133 **FAX** (0578) 755124
E-MAIL info@lolmopienza.it **WEBSITE** www.olmopienza.it

THE INITIAL IMPRESSION given by this solid stone building, set on a hillside overlooking the rolling hills of the Val d'Orcia towards Pienza, is a little stark. A few trees would soften the lines. Once inside, however, the elegant, comfortable sitting room, with its Oriental rugs, low beamed ceiling, antiques and glass-topped coffee table laden with books dispel any such feeling. When we visited, there was a fire roaring in the grate and Mozart playing softly in the background.

The spacious bedrooms and suites (two of which have fireplaces) are individually and stylishly decorated in smart country style with floral fabrics, fresh white cotton bedcovers, botanical prints, soft lighting and plenty of plants and dried flowers. One room has the floor-to-ceiling brick-grilled wall (now glassed in) that is so typical of Tuscan barns. The wrought iron fixtures throughout are by a local craftsman. Two suites have private terraces leading on to the large garden.

The pool has a wonderful view and the arched courtyard makes a pleasant spot for an aperitif.

~

NEARBY Siena (50 km); Pienza (7 km); Montepulciano (12 km).
LOCATION 7 km S of Pienza; follow signs to Montichiello; car parking
FOOD breakfast, dinner on request
PRICE €€
ROOMS 1 double, 5 suites and 1 self catering apartment, all with bath; all rooms have phone, TV, minibar, hairdrier, safe
FACILITIES sitting room, breakfast/dining room, garden, terraces, swimming pool
CREDIT CARDS AE, MC, V
DISABLED one ground floor bedroom
PETS not accepted
CLOSED mid Nov-end Mar
LANGUAGES French, English
PROPRIETOR Francesca Lindo

SIENA

PIENZA

IL CHIOSTRO DI PIENZA
~ FORMER MONASTERY ~

Corso Rossellino 26, Pienza, 53026 Siena
TEL (0578) 748400 **Fax** (0578) 748440
E-MAIL ilchiostrocdipienza@virgilio.it **WEBSITE** www.relaisilchiostrodipienza.com

IN THE MODEST WAY of Renaissance popes, Pius II re-named his home town of Corsignano after himself and made it a model of 15thC urban planning. So it is appropriate that the modern tourist-pilgrim should find lodgings in this stylishly converted monastery. The entrance is located at the back of the austere white cloister that gives the hotel its name and on to which half the rooms look; the other half face away, over the serenely magnificent hills of Val d'Orcia.

Many of the original features of the monks' cells have been retained: frescoed, vaulted ceilings and tiled floors. The furniture, however, breaks with monkish antiquity and concentrates on modern comfort without sinning against the character of the building. Bathrooms, though hardly spacious, are fully equipped.

The sitting rooms, with their old beamed ceilings, and the restaurant, give on to a delightful terrace garden, where a pool has recently been built - a great bonus in a town. There could be no more agreeable place for one's evening aperitif than its shady peace. A recent guest found the atmosphere, welcome and service faultless; 'I wouldn't mind moving in for life' she says.

~

NEARBY Palazzo Piccolomini, Duomo, Siena (52 km); Montepulciano.
LOCATION centre of town next to Palazzo Piccolomini; car parking outside walls
FOOD breakfast, lunch, dinner
PRICE €€€€
ROOMS 19 double and twin, 9 single, 9 suites, all with bath; all rooms have phone, TV, air conditioning, minibar, safe, hairdrier
FACILITIES sitting rooms, bar, restaurant, garden, swimming pool
CREDIT CARDS AE, DC, MC, V
DISABLED 2 adapted rooms
PETS accepted **CLOSED** Jan-Mar; restaurant Mon
LANGUAGES English
MANAGER Massimo Cicala

SIENA

PIENZA

LA SARACINA
~ COUNTRY GUESTHOUSE ~

Strada Statale 146, 53026 Pienza, Siena
TEL (0578) 748022 **FAX** (0578) 748018
E-MAIL info@lasaracina.it **WEBSITE** www.lasaracina.it

B Y THE TIME the McCobbs retired from La Saracina to return to the U.S.A. in 1996, they had created an extremely comfortable guesthouse. With the attention to detail that seems to be characteristic of foreigners who go into business, they turned an old stone farmhouse and its outbuildings, set in glorious countryside, into something special.

A sense of refinement and good taste pervades: the bedrooms, all with their own entrance from out of doors, are spacious and elegant, and suites have sitting areas. Antique furnishings mingle well with bright Ralph Lauren fabrics, and there is a distinct leaning towards American country style. The luxurious bathrooms are fitted with marble sinks and Jacuzzis - several are enormous. Breakfast is served in the winter garden or in a neat breakfast room. There is an attractive swimming pool surrounded by smooth lawns.

We have no reason to believe that the new young owner has not maintained the high standards of this upmarket place and that her enthusiasm and fresh approach have not been winning through. Reports please.

~

NEARBY Pienza (7 km); Montepulciano (6 km).
LOCATION 7 km from Pienza on Montepulciano road; car parking
FOOD breakfast
PRICE €€€
ROOMS 2 double, 3 suites and 1 self-catering apartment, all with bath or shower; all rooms have phone, TV, minibar
FACILITIES breakfast room, garden, swimming pool, tennis
CREDIT CARDS AE, MC, V
DISABLED no special facilities, but all rooms are on ground floor
PETS not accepted **CLOSED** never
LANGUAGES English, French
PROPRIETOR Simonetta Vessichelli

S I E N A

PIEVESCOLA DI CASOLE D'ELSA

RELAIS LA SUVERA
～ COUNTRY VILLA ～

Pievescola di Casole d'Elsa, 53030 Siena
TEL (0577) 960 300/1/2/3 **FAX** (0577) 960 220
E-MAIL lasuvera@lasuvera.it **WEBSITE** www.lasuvera.it

IN 1507, when Siena gave the castle of Suvera to Pope Julius II, he added an entire Renaissance villa on the same scale. It now belongs to Marchesi Ricci Paracciani and is one of the most extraordinary hotels in Italy.

Stone-built and three storeys high, in a panoramic position, the uncompromising lines of the fortress wing contrast with the delicate arched loggias, the villa's principal façade. To the side stands a 15thC church, and ornamental gardens carved up by precisely aligned gravel paths.

To do justice to the interiors would require a book in itself. A collector's fantasies come true? A display of aristocratic luxury? Or an essay in kitsch? Each room has a theme (the Pope's Room, the Savoy Room, the Angel's Room) and each theme has been pursued to its limits. Napoleon's Room is furnished in pure Empire style, hung with heavy drapes and contains a portrait of the brooding megalomaniac himself, surmounted by an Imperial Eagle. Rooms in the converted stables and farm house are (relatively) simpler and smaller. An elegant restaurant occupies the former olive-press.

～

NEARBY Siena (28 km); Florence (56 km).
LOCATION 28 km W of Siena, in its own grounds; car parking
FOOD breakfast, lunch, dinner
PRICE €€€€€
ROOMS 23 doubles, 12 suites, all with bath or shower, TV, phone, air conditioning
FACILITIES sitting rooms, breakfast room, restaurant, swimming pool, tennis, health centre with steam bath, Jacuzzi
CREDIT CARDS AE, DC, MC, V
DISABLED not suitable
PETS on request **CLOSED** Nov-April
LANGUAGES English, French, German, Spanish
PROPRIETOR Marchese Ricci Paracciani

SIENA

POGGIBONSI

VILLA SAN LUCCHESE
~ COUNTRY VILLA ~

Via San Lucchese 5, Poggibonsi, 53036 Siena
TEL (0577) 934231 **FAX** (0577) 934729
E-MAIL info@villasanlucchese.com **WEBSITE** www.villasanlucchese.com

DO NOT BE PUT OFF by nearby Poggibonsi, which, most people agree, is one of the ugliest towns in Tuscany. Lying halfway between Florence and Siena, visitors take one look at it from the motorway and speed on, or are forced to skirt it on the way to San Gimignano. However, its ugliness is contained, and once outside its environs, you are back in glorious Tuscan countryside, conscious only of cypresses, olives and vines – which is what you will also see from Villa San Lucchese's hilltop.

The villa is an elegant, 15thC cream-coloured building standing in its own park of sculpted hedges and swirling gravel paths. The interiors have been extensively refurbished to the standards of a four-star hotel, with perhaps more attention paid to modern comforts than to original style. Still, plenty of the character of the old villa remains, whether in the reception area with its heavy-beamed ceilings and low arches or in the dining-room's friezes and sloping roof. More colour would have been welcome in the bedrooms which, with their predominantly white tones, lacked vivacity and personality, even if spacious and comfortable.

~

NEARBY Siena (19 km); Florence (36 km); San Gimignano (13 km).
LOCATION 2 km S of Poggibonsi on hilltop in own grounds; car parking
FOOD breakfast, dinner
PRICE €-€€€€
ROOMS 34 double, 2 suite, all with bath or shower; all rooms have TV, phone, minibar, air conditioning
FACILITIES sitting rooms, restaurant, bar, garden, two swimming pools, tennis courts, bowls
CREDIT CARDS AE, MC, V
DISABLED no special facilities **PETS** not accepted **CLOSED** Mid Jan-mid Feb
LANGUAGES English, French, German
MANAGER Marcantonio Ninci

SIENA

RADDA IN CHIANTI

PODERE TERRENO
~ COUNTRY GUESTHOUSE ~

Via Terreno 21, Volpaia, Radda in Chianti, 53017 Siena
TEL (0577) 738312 **FAX** (0577) 738400
E-MAIL podereterreno@chiantinet.it **WEBSITE** www.podereterreno.it

AT PODERE TERRENO you will find everything you might expect from a family guesthouse in the heart of Chianti: a four-hundred year old farmhouse with views of vines and olive groves; delicious home cooking; and a genuinely friendly welcome.

The dining room on the upper floor is the centre of the house. As well as eating meals together at the long wooden table, guests can relax in front of the huge, traditional fireplace, its wooden mantle hung with cheerful ceramics and mounted antlers. The room is packed full of rural artifacts: burnished copper vessels hang from the wooden beams, a cupboard hollowed out of a tree trunk, shelves stacked with bottles of wine. Downstairs there is another sitting room. The bedrooms, all off a long corridor, are simply but well furnished, each named after a type of vine, their white plaster walls enlivened with coloured stencils of flowers and plants. Bathrooms are smallish, with slightly garish green tiling.

They make award-winning wine and, come evening, you can take your glass of red to the covered sitting area in the garden and watch the swallows swirling around the terracotta roofs. This is in our bottom price band; still one German reader complained that it was poor value for money.

~

NEARBY Siena (35 km); Florence (43 km).
LOCATION 5 km N of Radda in Chianti; car parking
FOOD breakfast, dinner
PRICE €
ROOMS 7 double, 6 with shower, 1 with bath
FACILITIES sitting room, dining room, terrace, table tennis; lake nearby
CREDIT CARDS AE, MC, V
DISABLED not suitable
PETS accepted
CLOSED never
LANGUAGES English, French, German
PROPRIETORS Marie-Sylvie Haniez

SIENA

RELAIS FATTORIA VIGNALE
~ COUNTRY HOTEL ~

Via Pianigiani 15, Radda in Chianti, 53017 Siena
TEL (0577) 738300 **FAX** (0577) 738592
E-MAIL vignale@vignale.it **WEBSITE** www.vignale.it

FATTORIA VIGNALE is not only in the heart of Chianti, it was here that in 1924, Baldassare Pianigiani created the famous black rooster symbol and the Consorzio Vino Chianti Classico, which to this day sets the standards for the production of Italy's most famous wine.

The hotel also sets high standards for itself. Under the management of the quietly efficient Silvia Kummer, you should find no unexpected hitches during your stay here. Decoration and furnishing are tasteful and restrained and blend well with the original character of the manor house. The sitting-rooms are subdued in character, with elegant modern sofas and Persian rugs. One is decorated with frescoed panels depicting rural scenes. The bedrooms, including the ones in the annex across the road, are all well furnished in a superior rustic style.

The building is situated on a slope, and while the front resembles a town house, the back, a couple of levels down, is more like a farmhouse. Here, under a leafy pergola, breakfast is served, and a little further away, with the same dramatic views, is the swimming pool. Everything we look for in a charming small hotel.

~

NEARBY Siena (28 km); San Gimignano (40 km); Firenze (45 km).
LOCATION just outside village, 28 km N of Siena; own grounds, ample car parking
FOOD breakfast, snacks
PRICE €€-€€€€
ROOMS 25 double, 4 single, all with bath or shower, phone, TV, heating. 9 of the rooms are in the annex across the road
FACILITIES 3 sitting rooms, breakfast room, bar, terrace, garden, swimming pool
CREDIT CARDS AE, MC, V
DISABLED lift, but no special facilities **PETS** not accepted
CLOSED 8th-26th Dec; 6th Jan-25th Mar **LANGUAGES** English, German, French
MANAGER Silvia Kummer

SIENA

SAN CASCIANO DEI BAGNI

SETTE QUERCE
~ VILLAGE GUESTHOUSE ~

53040 San Casciano dei Bagni, Siena
TEL (0578) 58174 **FAX** (0578) 58172
E-MAIL settequerce@krenet.it **WEBSITE** www.evols.it/settequerce

SEVERAL GENERATIONS of Daniela Boni's family have run the local bar in this tiny spa town, located high in the hills in a remote corner of southern Tuscany. The family business expanded in 1997 to include a delightful and original hotel, and most recently, the bar has extended into an excellent restaurant, a wine bar and pizzeria, and a gift shop selling beautiful, bright ceramics from Vietri.

The name derives from the fact that the rambling town house backs on to an oak wood. The contemporary interior design is a refreshing change from the Tuscan norm. At ground level, earth tones, vivid reds and pinks prevail. Bedrooms on the second floor are in sunny yellows and greens, and at the top, shades of blue predominate. The cheerful fabrics on chairs, curtains, cushions and duvets are by Designers Guild. The rooms are all dotted with ornaments (old irons, rustic ceramics, basket ware), while framed black-and-white photos depicting the history of the village decorate the walls. Each bedroom has a comfortable sitting area (compensating for the lack of public sitting room) and a cleverly-designed kitchenette. Bathrooms are immaculate and several have Jacuzzis.

~

NEARBY thermal baths; Pienza (40km); Orvieto (40 km); Montepulciano (40 km).
LOCATION on street just outside town; public car parking close by
FOOD breakfast
PRICE €€€-€€€€€
ROOMS 9 suites, all with bath and shower; all rooms have phone, TV, air conditioning, minibar
FACILITIES bar, terraces, restaurant (same management, nearby)
CREDIT CARDS AE, MC, V
DISABLED two adapted ground floor suites
PETS accepted if small
CLOSED 2 weeks in Jan
LANGUAGES English, French
PROPRIETORS Daniela, Maurizio and Silvestro Boni

SIENA

SAN GIMIGNANO

L'ANTICO POZZO
~ TOWN GUESTHOUSE ~

Via San Matteo 87, 53037 San Gimignano, Siena
TEL (0577) 942014 **FAX** (0577) 942117
E-MAIL info@anticopozzo.co **WEBSITE** www.anticopozzo.com

THE ANCIENT BRICK WELL in question (*pozzo* means well) is in the entrance hall of this fine, 15thC town house situated on one of the pedestrian streets leading up to San Gimignano's central Piazza del Duomo. The building was beautifully restored in 1990, and is now, in our view, possibly the best hotel in town.

A stone staircase leads up to the large first-floor bedrooms and the breakfast room, the latter known as the sala rosa thanks to its deep pink walls. The waxed and worn terracotta tiles on this floor are original, as are the high, beamed ceilings. Several rooms have delicate frescoes; in one, the walls and ceiling are entirely painted with garlands of flowers and elegant, dancing figures.

Rooms on the upper floors are smaller, but still most attractive. Those at the top have attic ceilings and views of the famous towers or countryside to compensate for their small size.

Furnishings throughout are in simple good taste; carefully-chosen antiques mix well with the wrought iron beds; colours are muted. A pretty, walled terrace is an added bonus.

~

NEARBY Cathedral; Museo Civico; Torre Grossa.
LOCATION on pedestrian street in centre of town with public parking (300 m)
FOOD breakfast
PRICE €€-€€€
ROOMS 1 single and 17 doubles, all with bath or shower, phone, TV, radio, air conditioning, minibar
FACILITIES bar, terrace, breakfast room
CREDIT CARDS AE, DC, MC, V
DISABLED 2 adapted rooms and lift **PETS** not accepted
CLOSED 6 weeks in winter **LANGUAGES** English, German, Spanish
PROPRIETOR Emanuele Marro L'Olmo

SIENA

CASALE DEL COTONE
~ COUNTRY GUESTHOUSE ~

Cellole 59, San Gimignano, 53037 Siena
TEL & Fax (0577) 943236
E-MAIL info@casaledelcotone.com **WEBSITE** www.casaledelcotone.com

AN IMPRESSIVELY RESTORED farmhouse that has been decorated with taste to make it one of the finer bed and breakfasts in the San Gimignano area. The house, a long, low building with small brown-shuttered windows and the occasional external stairway, was once used as a hunting lodge, and in the breakfast room are the remains of a fresco depicting a deer in flight and a pheasant. Another farmhouse has recently been converted on the estate - the Rocca degli Olivi - beautifully situated, like the main farmhouse, and surrounded by vineyards and olive groves.

Great care has been taken with both the interiors and exteriors. Outside are well-tended gardens with gravel paths and neatly kept, colourful flowerbeds, and the main house is so positioned that even on a torrid August evening you will catch a cool breeze sitting there.

On the ground floor is the sitting room and breakfast area; in fine weather, breakfast is served in the garden. We were impressed with the furniture and decoration, using a few well-chosen antiques to set off the fine proportions of the rooms. The bedrooms have a similar, uncluttered, tasteful ambience, conducive to the peaceful, almost hushed atmosphere.

~

NEARBY Siena (35 km); Florence (50 km); Volterra (28 km).
LOCATION 2 km N of San Gimignano on the road to Certaldo; own grounds, ample car parking
FOOD breakfast, snacks
PRICE €-€€
ROOMS 10 double, 2 apartments, all with bath and shower; all rooms have satellite TV, hairdrier, minibar, phone
FACILITIES sitting room, bar, garden
CREDIT CARDS not accepted
DISABLED one suitable room
PETS not accepted
CLOSED Nov-Jan **LANGUAGES** English, French
PROPRIETOR Alessandro Martelli

SIENA

SAN GIMIGNANO

LE RENAIE
~ COUNTRY HOTEL ~

Pancole, San Gimignano, 53037 Siena
TEL (0577) 955044 **FAX** (0577) 955126
E-MAIL lerenaie@tuscany.net **WEBSITE** www.tuscany.net/lerenaie

L E RENAIE IS THE SISTER HOTEL of the nearby Villa San Paolo (page 138) and in some ways might be considered the poor relation, with a more modest approach to furnishing and decoration, but with the advantage of lower prices. The building is no architectural masterpiece, but a typical example of a modern rustic construction: a covered terrace framed by brick arches where, in fine weather, breakfast and dinner are served; French windows that open directly on to the private balconies belonging to some of the bedrooms.

Inside, modern terracotta flooring and cane furniture make for a light, fresh atmosphere. The restaurant, Da Leonetto, is popular with locals (especially for large functions) but gets mixed notices from reporters. Upstairs are the bedrooms which have a mixture of modern, built-in furniture and reproduction rustic.

Guests seem to appreciate the peaceful location, the full range of hotel services (including a swimming pool and access to the tennis court of Villa San Paolo) and the very reasonable prices. A useful place to base yourself for a few days if you are thinking of combining city touring with days by the swimming pool.

NEARBY San Gimignano (5 km); Siena (38 km); Volterra.
LOCATION 6 km N of San Gimignano, off road to Certaldo; private car parking
FOOD breakfast, lunch, dinner
PRICE €-€€
ROOMS 24 double, 1 single, all with bath or shower, phone, TV, air conditioning, safe, minibar
FACILITIES sitting area, restaurant, garden, swimming pool
CREDIT CARDS AE, DC, MC, V
DISABLED no special facilities **PETS** not in public areas
CLOSED Nov **LANGUAGES** English, German, French
PROPRIETOR Leonetto Sabatini

SIENA

SAN GIMIGNANO

VILLA SAN PAOLO
~ COUNTRY VILLA ~

Strada per Certaldo, San Gimignano, 53037 Siena
TEL (0577) 955100 **FAX** (0577) 955113
E-MAIL info@villasanpaolo.com **WEBSITE** www.villasanpaolo.com

Villa San Paolo has changed almost beyond recognition since it appeared in the last edition of our guide, leaving us unsure whether to include it. Recently the owners have enormously increased its size by adding a new borgo, bringing the total number of rooms to seventy eight - well outside our usual criteria. But the place still retains its atmosphere and feels like a small hotel despite its sophisticated facilities.

The villa is not particularly Tuscan in style, and inside, a lightness of touch in the choice of colours and furnishings gives it a welcome individuality and freshness. Surrounded by cypresses and olives, and with a view of San Gimignano from the swimming pool, you are in no doubt about where you are as you relax in this tranquil setting.

In the main part of the villa on the ground floor are the foyer and public rooms where modern cane furniture is mixed with antiques. Bedrooms are on the two floors above, and those just below the roof have smallish windows. A common style has been followed with colour co-ordination of carpets, furniture and fabrics. Outside are the well-tended gardens, with gravel paths skirted by curling box-hedges under tall umbrella pines. A small ornamental fountain gurgles soothingly. The swimming pool has its own bar and a covered terrace where breakfast is served. As we went to press there were plans to build a spa, with treatments based on local, natural products.

~

NEARBY San Gimignano (5 km); Siena (38 km).
LOCATION 5 km N of SanGimignano on the road to Certaldo; private car parking
FOOD breakfast, snacks
PRICE €€€
ROOMS 78 rooms all with bath or shower; all rooms have phone, satellite TV, minibar, safe, air conditioning, internet
FACILITIES sitting room, breakfast room, bar, conference facilities, garden, swimming pool, tennis, billiards, bikes **CREDIT CARDS** AE, DC, MC, V
DISABLED adapted rooms **PETS** not accepted **CLOSED** 8 Jan-Feb/Mar
LANGUAGES English, French,German **MANAGER** Remo Squarcia

SIENA

VILLA ARCENO
~ COUNTRY VILLA ~

Arceno, San Gusme, Castelnuovo Berardenga, 53010 Siena
TEL (0577) 359292 **FAX** (0577) 359276
WEBSITE www.jpmoser.com/relaisvillaarceno.html

VILLA ARCENO ORIGINALLY served as a hunting lodge for a Tuscan noble family, but 'lodge' is too humble a word to describe this aristocratic building. A long private road winds through the thousand-hectare estate (which has many farmhouses converted into apartments) to the square, rigidly symmetrical villa with its overhanging eaves, surrounded by lawns, gravel paths and flower-filled terracotta urns. In front of the villa is a separate, walled park in the Romantic style, with shady paths leading down to a small lake.

Inside, a cool, elegant style prevails: off-white walls and vaulted ceilings contrast with the warmth of terracotta floors (strewn with Persian carpets), reproduction antique furniture and light yellow drapes. The atmosphere is formal, but not stiffly so: the highly professional staff make guests feel more than welcome.

Upstairs, the guest-rooms which are all light and spacious, have been individually decorated. Particularly attractive is the suite, which has a bay of three arched windows. Some rooms have their own terraces. You should also ask to see the spiral stairway of the central tower that finishes in a rooftop gazebo.

~

NEARBY Siena (30 km); Florence (90 km).
LOCATION 30 km NE of Siena in its own estate; ample car parking
FOOD breakfast, lunch, dinner
PRICE €€€-€€€€
ROOMS 16 double, all with bath, phone, TV, mini bar, air conditioning
FACILITIES sitting rooms, restaurant, gardens, tennis, swimming pool, bikes
CREDIT CARDS AE, DC, MC, V
DISABLED not suitable **PETS** small dogs, but check first
CLOSED mid Nov-mid Mar
LANGUAGES English, French, German
PROPRIETOR Gualtiero Mancini

SIENA

SIENA

CERTOSA DI MAGGIANO
~ CONVERTED MONASTERY ~

Via Certosa 82, Siena 53100
TEL (0577) 288180 **FAX** (0577) 288189
E-MAIL info@certosadimaggiano.it **WEBSITE** www.certosadimaggiano.com

THOUGH IT LIES in the suburbs of Siena, this former Carthusian monastery – the oldest in Tuscany – has the benefit of its own large park and a luxuriously peaceful atmosphere. Although it is expensive, it is not swanky. The emphasis is on calm elegance and discreet service.

If the decoration of the bedrooms is disappointing, it is only because they do not live up to the ravishing public rooms. Guests can help themselves to drinks in the book-lined library, play backgammon or chess in a little ante-room or relax in the lovely sitting room. The fact that this was formerly the family home of the hotel's cultured owners is reflected in the country house atmosphere, with fresh flower arrangements just about everywhere. Excellent modern haute cuisine dishes are served with some ceremony in the pretty dining room, in the tranquil 14thC cloisters or under the arcades by the swimming pool.

Bear in mind that you will have to explore Siena by bus – it's too far to walk, and parking is almost impossible in the centre.

~

NEARBY Siena sights; San Gimignano (40 km); Florence (58 km).
LOCATION 1 km SE of city centre and Porta Romana; in gardens, with car parking opposite entrance and garage available
FOOD breakfast, lunch, dinner
PRICE €€€€€
ROOMS 9 double, 8 suites; all with bath; all have central heating, TV, phone, radio
FACILITIES dining room, bar, library, sitting room; tennis, heated outdoor swimming pool, heliport
CREDIT CARDS AE, DC, MC, V
DISABLED access possible – 3 rooms on ground floor **PETS** not accepted
CLOSED Christmas, 9th Jan-9th Feb
MANAGER Margherita Grossi

SIENA

SIENA

PALAZZO RAVIZZA
~ TOWN HOTEL ~

Pian dei Mantellini 34, 53100 Siena
TEL (0577) 280462 **FAX** (0577) 221597
E-MAIL bureau@palazzoravizza.it **WEBSITE** www.palazzoravizza.it

SIENA IS NOTORIOUS for its dearth of decent hotels in the centre of town, so we were delighted to see that Palazzo Ravizza (which has featured in our all-Italy guide for some years) has undergone a facelift and is now a very pleasant place in which to stay. Fortunately, the old fashioned, slightly faded charm has not been sacrificed to modernisation. The bedrooms still have their heavy-at-times quirky period furniture and polished parquet or terracotta floors, but the fabrics have been smartened up and bathrooms are all shining new with heated towel rails. Some even have double Jacuzzis.

Downstairs, the public rooms (in part with smart black-and-white floor tiles) have pretty painted ceilings and comfortable arm chairs and sofas. There is a cosy library, a smart new bar and an elegantly-appointed dining room. The slightly overgrown garden at the back is a great asset providing a cool and shady respite from the city heat, and tables are invitingly laid outside for breakfast and dinner in the summer.

~

NEARBY The Cathedral, Ospedale Santa Maria della Scala.
LOCATION SW of the town centre in residential street with own car parking
FOOD breakfast, dinner
PRICE €-€€
ROOMS 35 doubles and twins; 5 suites; all with bath or shower; all rooms have phone, TV, minibar
FACILITIES sitting rooms, bar, restaurant, garden
CREDIT CARDS AE, DC, MC, V
DISABLED Lift **PETS** accepted
CLOSED never
LANGUAGES English, French, German
PROPRIETOR Francesco Grotanelli de Santi

SIENA

SINALUNGA

LOCANDA DELL'AMOROSA

~ COUNTRY INN ~

Sinalunga, 53048 Siena
TEL (0577) 677211 **FAX** (0577) 63200
E-MAIL mailbox@abitarelastoria.it **WEBSITE** www.abitarelastoria.it

IN A CORNER of the Siena province, which is not overburdened with quality hotels, the Locanda dell'Amorosa shines out. It is as romantic as it sounds: an elegant Renaissance villa-cum-village, within the remains of the 14thC walls.

The accommodation consists of apartments in the houses where peasants and farm-workers once lived, or in the bedrooms in the old family residence. They are cool, airy and pretty, with whitewashed walls, terracotta floors, antique furniture and Florentine curtains and bedspreads – as well as immaculate modern bathrooms.

The old stables, beamed and brick-walled, have been transformed into a delightful rustic (but pricey) restaurant serving modern interpretations of traditional Tuscan recipes, using ingredients from the estate, which also produces wine.

To complete the village, there is a little parish church with a lovely 15thC fresco of the Sienese school. With discreet, attentive service, the Locanda dell'Amorosa remains, in our view, a Mecca for romantics, and, in spite of being on the itinerary of many a small, up-market tour group, has not lost its charm.

~

NEARBY Siena (45 km); Arezzo (45 km); Chianti.
LOCATION 2 km S of Sinalunga; ample car parking
FOOD breakfast, lunch, dinner
PRICE €€€€
ROOMS 12 double, 4 suites, all with bathroom; all rooms have central heating, phone, colour TV, minibar, air conditioning
FACILITIES dining room, sitting room, bar, swimming pool
CREDIT CARDS AE, DC, MC, V
DISABLED access difficult **PETS** not accepted
CLOSED mid Jan-end Feb; restaurant only, Mon, Tue
MANAGER Carlo Citterio

SIENA

SOVICILLE

BORGO PRETALE
~ HILLSIDE HAMLET ~

Pretale, Rosia Sovicille, 53018 Siena
TEL (0577) 345401 **FAX** (0577) 345625
E-MAIL borgopret@ftbcc.it

ALONG, WINDING, unsurfaced road through wooded hills brings you to this group of grey stone houses clustered around a massive 12thC watch-tower. Local historians claim that it was part of a system of such towers, spread across the Sienese hills, all within line of sight, to communicate quickly any news of approaching invaders and to provide protection against their rampages. Nowadays, this civilized retreat offers a haven from the rampages of modern life.

Every detail has been considered in the restoration and decoration. The harshness of the medieval structure has been lessened by the use of well-chosen antiques, mellow lighting and rich, striped fabrics. A serenely beautiful 15thC carved wooden Madonna, bearing the Infant Christ, stands in a brick-framed niche.

Every bedroom contains a different blend of the same artful ingredients, each splendid in its own individual way, though we particularly liked those in the tower. The stylish restaurant serves a limited choice of dishes (but all well-prepared) and has an extensive wine list on which a sommelier can offer advice. And tucked away, close to the edge of the woods, is an inviting pool.

~

NEARBY Siena (20 km); San Gimignano (28 km).
LOCATION 20 km SE of Siena on quiet hillside; own car parking
FOOD breakfast, lunch
PRICE €€€€
ROOMS 32 double, 3 suites, all with bath or shower, phone, TV, minibar, air conditioning
FACILITIES sitting room, restaurant, bar, garden, swimming pool, tennis, sauna, archery
CREDIT CARDS all
DISABLED not suitable **PETS** not accepted
CLOSED 1st Nov-5th Apr **LANGUAGES** English, French German
DIRECTOR Daniele Rizzardini

SIENA

SOVICILLE

BORGO DI TOIANO
~ COUNTRY HOTEL ~

Toiano, Sovicille, 53018 Siena
TEL (0577) 314639 **FAX** (0577) 314641

MOST OF THE ABANDONED rural hamlets (*borgo*) that once housed small farming communities and have since been converted into distinctive hotels were, for protection's sake, located on steep hills or jumbled together behind secure walls. Borgo di Toiano, by contrast, has a pleasant open aspect: a few old stone houses, superbly restored, spread out across acres of stone and terracotta terraces, with views over the flat, cultivated valley to low hills on the horizon.

The terraces, to which many of the bedrooms have direct access, are dotted with rosebeds, flower pots and wrought iron garden furniture, so that breakfast can be enjoyed in the early morning sun. The main public rooms also maintain a spacious, uncluttered feel, with fine antiques and old rugs contrasting with the pristine restoration. Tapestries and modern paintings are set off nicely by the white walls and subtle lighting. The bedrooms maintain the same mixture of rustic and modern with the emphasis on simplicity and comfort, and we particularly recommend those with views.

Below the main group of houses, on the last terrace of this shallow-sloping location, is the swimming pool. ~

NEARBY Siena (12 km); San Gimignano (50 km).
LOCATION 12 km SW of Siena in its own grounds; car parking
FOOD breakfast
PRICE €€€-€€€€
ROOMS 7 double, 3 suites, all with shower or bath, phone, TV, minibar, air-conditioning
FACILITIES sitting room, bar, terraces, garden, swimming pool
CREDIT CARDS AE, DC, MC, V
DISABLED some adapted rooms with bathrooms **PETS** accepted
CLOSED Nov-Mar **LANGUAGES** English, French, German
MANAGER Pierluigi Pagni

SIENA

LA LOCANDA
~ COUNTRY GUESTHOUSE ~

Montanino, 53017 Radda in Chianti, Siena
TEL & FAX (0577) 738833
E MAIL info@locanda.com **WEBSITE** www.lalocanda.it

THE BEVILAQUAS (he Neapolitan, she Milanese) began their search for the ideal spot in which to set up their guesthouse seven years ago. In April 1999, what was once a collection of ruined farm buildings high up in the Chianti hills finally opened for business, and you would be hard pressed to find a more beautiful setting. At 600 metres above sea level, views from the terraces, garden, pool and some of the rooms are of layers of hills, striped with vines and shaded with woods; in the foreground is the ancient, mellow fortified hamlet of Volpaia.

The restoration of the pale stone buildings has been done with unerring good taste. Interiors, while maintaining many of the rustic features, have a refreshingly contemporary look, with an imaginative use of colour throughout to offset plenty of terracotta and wood. The comfortable bedrooms have an uncluttered feel, and the bathrooms are spacious and gleaming. One end of the long, sunny living room is dominated by a massive stone fireplace, and filled with colourfully-upholstered sofas and arm chairs.

~

NEARBY Florence (48km); Siena (38 km).
LOCATION 4 km west of Volpaia. From piazza in village, follow signs to hotel
FOOD breakfast, dinner on request
PRICE €€€-€€€€
ROOMS 6 doubles and I suite, all with bath and shower, phone, TV, and safe.
FACILITIES terraces, garden, swimming pool
CREDIT CARDS AE, DC, MC, V
DISABLED some ground floor bedrooms, but no special facilities
PETS not accepted
CLOSED mid Jan-mid March
LANGUAGES English, French
PROPRIETORS Guido and Martina Bevilaqua

SIENA

BUONCONVENTO

FATTORIA PIEVE A SALTI
FARM GUESTHOUSE

Pieve a Salti, Buonconvento, 53022 Siena

TEL & FAX (0577) 807244
E-MAIL info@pieveasalti.it
FOOD breakfast, lunch, dinner
PRICE €
CLOSED never

HERE IS AN APPEALING choice for those who like the outdoor life. Pieve a Salti is set in 550 hectares of farmland and hunting reserve which supplies its restaurant with olive oil, meat, game and cheeses. Comfortable rooms and apartments, in typical rustic Tuscan style – stone, brick, terracotta, old beamed ceilings, mahogany wardrobes – are distributed among the estate's farmhouses, some grouped around the main farm itself, others dotted around the estate. No less than six fishing ponds are available for anglers and a swimming pool for idlers. A recent addition is the health and beauty centre, with indoor pool, Turkish bath, sauna and gym. After fishing or walking, before dinner, you can have a massage.

CASTELLINA IN CHIANTI

VILLA CASALECCHI
COUNTRY VILLA

Casalecchi, Castellina in Chianti, 53011 Siena

TEL (0577) 740240
FAX (0577) 741111
E-MAIL casalecchi@tuscany.net
PRICE €€-€€€
CLOSED Oct-Mar

AN 18THC VILLA standing on a series of terraces between woods and vineyards, just south of Castellina. It's no architectural gem, but its secluded position and attractive location compensate for the exterior's somewhat austere appearance. Originally a hunting lodge, the interiors are furnished with heavy, bourgeois antiques, giving the place a hushed character. The dining room is frescoed with elegant old light fittings, and a more pleasant place in which to eat is the terrace with views of open countryside (breakfast, lunch and dinner available). Bedrooms are either in the villa or in the extension. There is a swimming pool, and below it a terrace where you can lie on a sun bed beside a vineyard. The glories of Chianti are on the doorstep.

SIENA

CASTELNUOVO BERARDENGA

PODERE COLLE AI LECCI

FARMHOUSE APARTMENTS

*San Gusme, Castelnuovo
Berardenga, 53010 Siena*

TEL (0577) 359084
FAX (0577) 358914
E-MAIL none
FOOD breakfast, lunch, dinner
PRICE €€
CLOSED never

THE ENTERPRISING DANISH OWNER of this old stone farmhouse, Brent W. Myhre, modernized this estate's wine production and now makes one of the finest Chianti Classicos (and two lesser ones). The house itself is classically Chianti in its location amidst vines, olives and cypresses. Some apartments have their own terraces; others have small private gardens. There are fine views of the Val d'Orcia. Naturally, wine and oil on sale. Colle ai Lecci means hill of oaks.

CASTEL SAN GIMIGNANO

LE VOLPAIE
SUBURBAN HOTEL

*Via Nuova 9, Castel San
Gimignano, 53030 Siena*

TEL (0577) 953140
FAX (0577) 953142
E-MAIL levolpaie@iol.it
WEBSITE www.hotelvolpaie.it
FOOD breakfast
PRICE €-€€
CLOSED 10 Nov-10 Mar

A SMALL MODERN HOTEL, with swimming pool, and not without hints of character, in the suburbs of the nondescript town of Castel San Gimignano. Set in spectacular Tuscan countryside, Le Volpaie is perfect for an overnight stop - or longer - if touring this popular area. (A car or motorbike is essential.) The friendly welcome from owners Anna and Luca Sozzi, the clean, comfortable rooms (many with their own balconies) and the attractive garden make this a place not to be overlooked. Readers heap praise on Anna's impressive buffet breakfast.

SIENA

COLLE VAL D'ELSA

BELVEDERE
COUNTRY VILLA

*Belvedere, Colle Val d'Elsa, 53034
Siena*

TEL (0577) 920966
FAX (0577) 924128
E-MAIL none
FOOD breakfast
PRICE €-€€
CLOSED never

THIS TIME-WORN OLD VILLA set in its own grounds operates chiefly as a restaurant (especially for weddings and other large functions). Owned by the Conti and Iannone families, it was originally the home of a Florentine aristocrat, Count Ceramelli. It is set in large, well-tended Italian gardens, where aromatic herbs are grown for chef Daniele to use in his superb traditional Tuscan dishes. The guest-book is full of appreciative comments, and they have now started a cookery school. The decoration is predominantly heavy rustic in style. Each of the 15 rooms has a view, and the busy nearby road is less of a nuisance since double-glazing was installed.

FONTERUTOLI

CASTELLO DI FONTERUTOLI
VILLAGE APARTMENTS

*Fonterutoli, Castellina in
Chianti, 53011 Siena*

TEL (0577) 73571
FAX (0577) 735757
E-MAIL fonterutoli@fonterutoli.it
FOOD self-catering
PRICE €
CLOSED never

IN THE HEART of Chianti Classico, on the wine estate of the Mazzei family, cultivators of vines and producers of wine for more than 500 years, this quaint stone-built village contains some stylishly converted and furnished apartments for weekly rent. Decorated by the Marchesa in country-house style with family paintings on the walls and antique furniture, the apartments are in cottages, grouped around the family villa on the main square. The village is secluded despite the nearby Chiantigiana. There's a good restaurant here that also sells local produce, and guests can tour the estate wine cellars and vineyards, and taste the award winning wines. There is a swimming pool.

SIENA

GAIOLE IN CHIANTI

CASTELLO DI TORNANO
CASTLE HOTEL

Lecchi, Gaiole in Chianti, 53013 Siena

TEL (0577) 746067
FAX (0577) 746094
E-MAIL info@castelloditornano.it
WEBSITE www.castelloditornano.it
FOOD breakfast, lunch, dinner
PRICE €€€ **CLOSED** never

ONE OF THE COUNTLESS DEFENCE and watchtowers that dot Tuscany and solidly built in grey stone with commanding views of the surrounding countryside, the Castello di Tornano has undergone something of a transformation recently. There are still self-catering apartments for rent in an adjoining farmhouse, but these are rather drab compared to the luxourious rooms that are now available in the castle and tower itself. The style is rather theatrical with a medieval feel; deep red brocaded fabrics, mezza corona beds, elaborated wrought iron light fittings, luxourious (unmedieval) bathrooms. The restaurant serves Tuscan specialities and there is a hot tub on the top of the tower.

MONTEFOLLONICO

LA CHIUSA
COUNTRY GUESTHOUSE

Via della Madonnina 88, 53040 Montefollonico, Siena

TEL (0577) 669668
FAX (0577) 669593
E-MAIL info@ristorantelachiusa.it
WEBSITE www.ristorantelachiusa.it
FOOD breakfast, lunch, dinner
PRICE €€€
CLOSED Jan-Mar; restaurant Tue

NOT A FEW OF THE BETTER hotels in this guide started as restaurants, over the years acquiring a few rooms for overnight stays. In general, the restaurant remains the centre of the enterprise. La Chiusa, a stone farmhouse and olive press, is no exception, but guests' comfort is far from secondary. Greatest care has been taken over the bedrooms: elegant and spacious, all are individually furnished with antiques. There are colourful rugs on terracotta tiles, modern lamps provide artful lighting and bathrooms are among the best we have seen. Meals in the elegant restaurant are gastronomic experiences that venture beyond the merely regional, despite being based on ingredients from the vegetable garden.

SIENA

MONTORIO

SELF-CATERING APARTMENTS

Strada per Pienza 2, 53045
Montepulciano, Siena

TEL (0578) 717442
FAX (0578) 715456
E-MAIL info@montorio.com
WEBSITE www.montorio.com
FOOD breakfast, by request
PRICE €-€€€
CLOSED mid Nov-end Jan

THIS GROUP OF FIVE self-catering apartments makes it into the guide for the first time this edition as much as for its exceptional location as anything else. It perches on the summit of a steep little hill - more of a mound - outside Montepulciano, and it overlooks the spectacular church of San Biagio on its even more amazing site. The apartments are clean, adequately equipped and quite nicely furnished; you could be comfortable here for a week, with not only the wine town of Montepulciano to explore on your doorstep, but nearby Pienza and other sites of southern Tuscany. The most expensive apartment has 390-degree views. We enjoyed relaxing in the well-maintained garden with, of course, great views. No pool.

IL RICCIO

TOWN GUESTHOUSE

Via Talosa 21, Montepulciano, 53045
Siena

TEL (0578) 757713
FAX (0578) 757713
E-MAIL info@ilriccio.net
FOOD breakfast
PRICE €
CLOSED first 10 days in June, first 10 days in Nov

LOCATED RIGHT IN THE CENTRE of the historic town of Montepulciano, near the Piazza Grande, in an old building going back to the 13thC. Although recent restoration has unfortunately removed much of the original character, some features, including the medieval entrance, courtyard and cloisters, remain intact. It has been in the Caroti family for many years, and the typically Italian warmth and hospitality of its present owners, Giorgio and Ivana, bring guests back here year after year. Bedrooms tend to be small, but beds are large and comfortable, and some rooms have impressive views of the city. Ask for one of these when you book. A friendly, convenient guesthouse that offers great value for money.

SIENA

MONTERIGGIONI

CASTEL PIETRAIO

CASTLE APARTMENTS

Castel Pietraio, Monteriggioni, 53035 Siena

TEL (0577) 301038
FAX (051) 221376
E-MAIL m.delnero@tin.it
FOOD self-catering
PRICE ©©© **CLOSED** never

SOLID APARTMENTS for Tuscan enthusiasts are split between this imposing, even forbidding grey medieval stone structure, originally one of Siena's defensive outposts, and a farmhouse on the estate. The comfortable double rooms are in the cosier 17thC lodge. The surrounding park and the pool have been attractively landscaped and are well-maintained. A few kilometers away are the more elegant defences of Monteriggioni, arguably Tuscany's most perfect fortified village. Not much to do locally, but it makes a good base for Siena, Florence, San Gimignano and Volterra.

MONTICIANO

LOCANDA DEL PONTE

COUNTRY HOTEL

Ponte a Macereto, Monticiano, 53015 Siena

TEL (0577) 757108
FAX (0577) 757110
FOOD breakfast, lunch, dinner
E-MAIL info@locandadelponte.it
PRICE ©©-©©©
CLOSED Feb

THIS 17TH CENTURY inn was in the old days a stopping point for the Italian post (nobody knows where it stops now). The best of its 23 rooms (all with bath or shower, phone, TV, minibar and air conditioning) look on to the River Merse and the ruined bridge that gave the locanda its name, now the site of the hotel's private river beach. By all accounts it is an excellent, low-key place that may persuade visitors for more than just an overnight stay, especially as it is not far from Siena. One couple describe arriving unannounced, lost and fed up, very late at night, and being welcomed with plates of cold meat and cheese before being shown to their spotlessly clean and elegantly rustic room.

SIENA

MONTI IN CHIANTI

LOCANDA DEL MULINO

FARM GUESTHOUSE

Mulino delle Bagnaie, Monti in Chianti, 53010 Siena

TEL & FAX (0577) 747103
E-MAIL
info@locandadelmulino.com
FOOD breakfast, dinner
PRICE € **CLOSED** Nov-Mar

AN OLD STONE and shuttered mill in the lush Val d'Esse has been attractively converted to make this restaurant with rooms, situated between a stream and a road. Fortunately most of the bedrooms look on to the quieter side, and are appealingly decorated in pale shades with wrought iron beds and comfortable Tuscan furniture. Downstairs is a pleasant sitting room for guests and a good-value restaurant serving Tuscan and Umbrian specialities, decorated with old terracotta pots and dried flowers. The lovely Etruscan hill town of Cortona is 7km away. Swimming pool.

QUERCEGROSSA

MULINO DI QUERCEGROSSA

COUNTRY GUESTHOUSE

Via Chiantigiana, Quercegrossa, 53011 Siena

TEL & FAX (0577) 328129
E-MAIL none
FOOD breakfast, dinner
PRICE €
CLOSED Jan-mid Mar

A CONVERTED MILL, off the Chiantigiana (the old Florence-Siena road) surrounded by paved and terraced gardens. Locally well-known for its large restaurant and ice-cream parlour, both of which make for a lively atmosphere. The restaurant is highly regarded for its home-made pasta, grilled meat and excellent service. One recent reporter especially recommends the Florentine steak for two. Prices are very reasonable, and the furnishing is a good example of the modern 'rustic' style. Only 8 km from Siena and an hour's drive from Florence.

SIENA

RADDA IN CHIANTI

CASTELLO DI VOLPAIA

COUNTRY APARTMENTS

Volpaia, 53017 Radda in Chiani, Siena

TEL (0577) 738066
FAX (0577) 738619
E-MAIL info@volpaia.com
FOOD breakfast
PRICE ©© **CLOSED** never

FORTIFIED HILLTOP VILLAGE in deepest Chianti, now sadly 'discovered' by tourists. It produces some prestigious wines, and offers a few compact apartments. Nearby is the Podere Casetto, more spacious, and with private garden and pool. A quaint bar/grocery in the village sells everyday essentials, local produce and snacks. Volpaia is located on the minor road leading north from Radda in Chianti and could be a useful base for visits to Siena. Good country walks from the village.

ROCCA D'ORCIA

LA CISTERNA NEL BORGO

FORMER COACH-HOUSE

Roccia d'Orcia, 53027 Siena

TEL (0577) 887280
FAX (0577) 955102
E-MAIL none
FOOD breakfast, dinner
PRICE ©©
CLOSED Nov-Mar

CLOSE TO THE THERMAL SPRINGS of Bagno Vignoni and not far from Pienza, you will find, in the central *piazza* of this well-preserved medieval hamlet, overlooking the ancient well, the restaurant Cisterna nel Borgo, which, as well as serving delicious local food, also has a few stylishly decorated bedrooms for visitors. It was built in the early 18thC as a coaching inn, and its origins are still obvious in the handsome vaulted dining room which retains its old tiled floor and immense wooden counter. The cuisine is regional and concentrates on meat (the bistecca alla fiorentina is excellent); other specialities incorporate porcini, and fresh ricotta.

SIENA

SAN GIMIGNANO

IL CASOLARE DI LIBBIANO

COUNTRY GUESTHOUSE

Libbiano 3, San Gimignano, 53037 Siena

TEL & FAX (0577) 946002
E-MAIL none
WEBSITE www.casolare.libbiano.it
FOOD breakfast, dinner
PRICE €€ **CLOSED** Nov-Mar

CAREFULLY RESTORED and tastefully furnished old farmhouse which combines the advantages of country seclusion with easy access to San Gimignano and Siena. Overlooking vineyards and olive groves (it was once an olive oil farm), the current owners, Berta and Andrea, have decorated the house in simple, elegant Tuscan style. In both bedrooms and reception rooms, plain white walls and antique furniture complement the terracotta-tiled floors and beamed or delicately frescoed ceilings. If you don't feel like exploring, there is a swimming pool surrounded by comfortable sun-loungers, plenty of places to sit and relax, and excellent local cuisine on the spot. Bikes for hire.

SAN GIMIGNANO

LA FORNACE DI RACCIANO

CONVERTED FARMHOUSE

Racciano 6, San Gimignano, 53037 Siena

TEL & FAX (0577) 942156
E-MAIL info@lafornacediracciano.it
FOOD breakfast
PRICE €-€€
CLOSED Nov-Feb (except Christmas)

THE BEST FEATURE of this comfortable converted farmhouse, managed by a young family, and one that would be hard to beat on any level, is its marvellous view of the famous towers of San Gimignano. The farmhouse sits in countryside just outside the town, and its owners have wisely stuck to the well-tried formula of terracotta, beams, brick and plaster, with no fancy touches. Perhaps too few for some: rooms are large, white-walled, beamed and terracotta-floored and a little sparsely furnished, while the cavernous breakfast room (the old hay loft) has a large fireplace and little tables and chairs dotted about. Prices are reasonable, and the alluring swimming pool makes it an excellent bargain for this popular area.

SIENA

IL MATTONE
FARM GUESTHOUSE

Mattone (strada per Ulignano),
San Gimignano, 53037 Siena

TEL & FAX (0577) 950075
E-MAIL none
WEBSITE
www.agitourismoilmattone.it
FOOD breakfast
PRICE €-€€
CLOSED never

O N A HILL, 5 KILOMETRES north-east of San Gimignano, with panoramic
views, Il Mattone is a wine- and olive-producing agriturismo. Two farm
buildings have been turned into a pleasant arrangement of bedrooms and
apartments with their own little gardens, all sharing a kitchen, dining and
sitting area. Swimming pool and tennis court. Views. Good walking; riding
stables 1.5 km; bowling; and a mini Classical style auditorium for local
concerts and other events.

MONCHINO
COUNTRY GUESTHOUSE

Casale 12, San Gimignano,
53037 Siena

TEL (0577) 941136
FAX (0577) 943042
E-MAIL none
FOOD breakfast
PRICE €
CLOSED Dec-Feb

A DIRT TRACK BRINGS YOU to this old farmhouse (parts of which date back
to the 15thC), about 3 km east of San Gimignano. The neat garden,
filled with flower pots, has views over the vines to the town. The owners
pride themselves on giving guests a warm welcome, and the simple, light
rooms in the converted hay barn are adequate, bearing in mind their reasonable price. They make their own Vernaccia white wine, Chianti, grappa and olive oil, all of which are, inevitably, on sale. Wine tastings organized for groups. Archery.

SIENA

SAN GIMIGNANO

PODERE MONTESE
FARM GUESTHOUSE

Fugnano, Via Cellole 11, San Gimignano, 53037 Siena

TEL (0577) 941127
FAX (0577) 907350/938856
E-MAIL montese@tuscany.net
WEBSITE
www.tuscany.net/montese
PRICE (€) **CLOSED** Nov-Mar

YET ANOTHER GUESTHOUSE (breakfast only) in the orbit of San Gimignano, dramatically situated on a hillside 1.5 km north of San Gimignano. Visitors will appreciate the warm welcome and complete peace and quiet of Podere Montese as well as its swimming pool complete with panoramic view. Rooms are modest but pleasant, with white-tiled floors and modern rustic furniture.There's a large sitting room with fireplace, and two kitchens are for guests' use. Some 100 m from the main house is an apartment sleeping three people. The garden terrace makes a pleasant spot. You can keep busy here, with mountain bike rental 1 km away; fishing and tennis at 5 km; and riding at 6 km.

SAN GIMIGNANO

PODERE VILLUZZA
COUNTRY BED AND BREAKFAST

Strada 25, San Gimignano, 53037 Siena

TEL (0577) 940585
FAX (0577) 942247
E-MAIL viluzza@tin.it
FOOD breakfast, dinner
PRICE (€)(€) **CLOSED** never

A SIMPLE FARMHOUSE with a few rooms and small apartments to offer guests, at the end of an unsurfaced road 3 km north of San Gimignano. Podere Villuzza is very much a working farm, with vines growing practically to the door and spectacular views of the surrounding hills. Although there is nothing fancy about the accomodation, the rustic-style rooms are attractive, with their beams, solid wooden furniture and beds covered in patchwork quilts. As well as a swimming pool and table tennis, there are mountain bikes for hire and riding stables 5km away. Pleasant, honest hospitality from hosts, Gianni and Sandra, in a geniune rural setting and at reasonable prices.

SIENA

SAN MICHELE
FARM GUESTHOUSE

Strada 14, San Gimignano, 53037 Siena

TEL & FAX (0577) 940596
E-MAIL info@sanmichelehotel.it
WEBSITE www.sanmichelehotel.it
FOOD breakfast
PRICE €
CLOSED 8 Jan-15 Mar

BRIGHT, UP-TO-DATE interiors and clean public areas quickly establish the unfussy style of this hotel. Bedrooms, not very large, nor with much character, are nonetheless pleasant and well furnished. Each has a new, modern bathroom. Rooms available for the disabled. Enjoyment of the garden diminished somewhat by the nearby road, but there are enough shady spots for stretching out in privacy and the swimming pool has great views. Run by two sisters, Paola and Roberta, with a warm welcome. About 1.5 km from San Gimignano.

VILLA BACIOLO
FORMER FARMHOUSE

San Donato, San Gimignano, 53037 Siena

TEL & FAX (0577) 942233
E-MAIL none
FOOD breakfast
PRICE €
CLOSED Nov-Mar

REASONABLY PRICED, simple guesthouse only 4 km from San Gimignano, with a shady garden and the inevitable view which you can enjoy with your breakfast on the terrace. Restoration of this originally medieval building has been extensive, but sensitive and unobtrusive. Impressive brick vaulted ceilings. Bedrooms are surprisingly stylish, given the reasonable prices. Two small apartments complete the accommodation. A pleasant garden contains the swimming pool. You're 4 km from San Gimignano, 30 km from Siena, and if you need more to amuse you, ask for the walking map highlighting ancient paths and tracks in the vicinity.

SIENA

SAN GIMIGNANO

VILLA BELVEDERE
COUNTRY HOTEL

Via Dante 14, San Gimignano, 53037 Siena

TEL (0577) 940539
FAX (0577) 940327
E-MAIL hotel.villa.belvedere
@tin.it **FOOD** breakfast, dinner
PRICE € **CLOSED** never

A LATE 19THC ART NOUVEAU VILLA redecorated in a light, contemporary style which will appeal to those who prefer modern comfort to time-worn individuality. Rooms are all in soothing pastel colours, and though harmonious, the bedrooms are somewhat bland and characterless. The gardens are lush and well laid out, with palms, olives, cypresses and rosemary bushes, but too close to a busy road for true seclusion. If you can block out the noise from the road, there are plenty of small tables and chairs, shaded by trees or parasols, where you can sit and relax. The swimming pool is a bonus at these reasonable prices.

SARTEANO

LE ANFORE
COUNTRY GUESTHOUSE

Via di Chiusi 30, 53047 Sarteano, Siena

TEL (0578) 265969
FAX (0578) 265521
E-MAIL manola@intuscany.net
WEBSITE www.balzarini.it
FOOD breakfast, dinner
PRICE €€
CLOSED 7-30 Nov

A N OLD FARMHOUSE in the corner of Tuscany surrounding Sarteano and Cetona, restored, we must admit, without special flair or style (there was a gnome near the front door when we visited). But it has a pleasantly rustic atmosphere, there's a huge fireplace in the brick-arched living room, its in unspoilt countryside, and its a useful base for exploring the Val d'Orcia. Prices are reasonable. Bedrooms (polished parquet floors and oriental rugs) are mostly spacious and a little more stylish than the public rooms. Bathrooms are smartly tiled and well lit. Outside, there is plenty to do, with a big pool in the garden, and tennis and riding (of all standards) nearby. Reasonably close to Pienza and Montepulciano.

SIENA

SANTA CHIARA

CONVERTED CONVENT

*Piazza Santa Chiara, Sarteano,
53047 Siena*

TEL (0578) 265412
FAX (0578) 266849
E-MAIL rsc@cyber.dada.it
WEBSITE www.cybermarket.it/rsc
FOOD breakfast, dinner
PRICE €€-€€€
CLOSED 10 days in Feb and Nov

A 16THC MONASTERY stylishly converted into a restaurant and hotel. The walled garden has an uninterrupted view of the Valdichiana. Furnishings and decoration show an eclectic mix of styles, with the rustic dominant. There are four double rooms, two that sleep three people and a suite that has views across to Val di Chiana and Lake Trasimeno. It was originally accommodation for the convent mother, with an old bread oven still in place. The restaurant, spanned by brick arches, concentrates on Tuscan cooking, with the emphasis on ingredients such as truffles and porcini mushrooms. Santa Chiara holds cookery classes, organized on a weekly basis.

SANTA CATERINA

TOWN HOTEL

*Via Enea Silvio Piccolomini 7,
53100 Siena*

TEL (0577) 221105
FAX (0577) 271087
E-MAIL info@hscsiena
WEBSITE www.hscsiena.it
PRICE €€ **CLOSED** never

A N 18THC PATRICIAN villa converted effortlessly, as usual in these parts, into an elegant but friendly, perhaps even cosy, small (breakfast-only) hotel. It's located just a few metres from Siena's Porta Romana, so you're a healthy walk from the city centre. In recent years it's been enlarged, but retains much of its intimate character. Bedrooms on the garden side enjoy some peace, while those on the street side have some sound proofing. Well chosen antiques are in keeping with the building's character, and original features such as marble fireplaces or frescoes run shoulders with tastefully chosen fabrics (nothing too contemporary, though). There's a considerable garden; breakfast served outside on the terrace.

SIENA

SIENA

VILLA SCAC-CIAPENSIERI

TOWN VILLA

Via di Scacciapensieri 10, 53100 Siena

TEL (0577) 41441
E-MAIL villasca@tin.it
FOOD breakfast
PRICE €€-€€€
CLOSED Jan-mid Mar

O N A HILLTOP 2 km north-east of Siena's historic centre, this 19th centu-ry villa has views of both the city's enchanting skyline and the peace-ful Tuscan countryside. A formal garden with box hedges keeps at bay any recent suburban development, and as for getting to town, there is a public bus service every 15 minutes from the gate. The villa is surrounded by its own large park and gardens, with a shady terrace and a swimming pool (not heated, and open from June until September), tennis court and park-ing. The bedrooms, with beamed and decorated ceilings, are large and simply furnished. A reader comments that the rooms are 'among the loveliest in Italy.'

PERUGIA

ASPROLI

POGGIO D'ASPROLI
~ COUNTRY GUESTHOUSE ~

Asproli 7, 06059 Todi, Perugia
TEL & FAX (075) 8853385
E-MAIL poggio@todi.net **WEBSITE** www.todi.net/poggio

IF YOU ARE TIRED of Naples, you may not be tired of life – just in need of peace and quiet. Such was the case with Bruno Pagliari, so he sold his large southern hotel to continue his career as an artist in the tranquillity of Umbria's leafy valleys. But the tradition of hospitality remained, and he has opened up his hillside farmhouse so that his guests can also enjoy this oasis.

The rambling building of local stone is packed full of an arresting mixture of antiques and Bruno's own modern art. The main sitting room, with its great fireplace and white couches, is flanked by a long terrace where one can eat or just relax, listening to the birdsong of the wooded hills.

In the rest of the house, stone and brick arches frame decoratively painted doors and parchment-shaded lights illuminate old coloured wooden carvings. The bedrooms will inspire many a pleasant dream.

The atmosphere is hushed, but in a relaxed rather than reverent manner and, birdsong aside, the only sound is of operatic arias gently playing in the background.

~

NEARBY Todi (7 km); Orvieto (29 km).
LOCATION country house in its own grounds
FOOD breakfast; dinner on request
PRICE €€
ROOMS 7 double, 2 suite all with shower or bath, phone, heating
FACILITIES pool, garden, terrace, sitting room
CREDIT CARDS AE, MC, V
DISABLED difficult
PETS not accepted
CLOSED Jan-Feb
LANGUAGES English, French, German
PROPRIETOR Bruno Pagliari

PERUGIA

LE SILVE
~ COUNTRY HOTEL ~

Armenzano, 06081 Assisi, Perugia
TEL (075) 8019000 **FAX** (075) 8019005
E-MAIL hotellesilve@tin.it **WEBSITE** www.lesilve.it

EVEN IF YOU ARE NOT PLANNING to stay at this sophisticated gem, the road up to Le Silve is worth exploring for its own rewards – or perhaps avoiding if you are the nervous sort. It winds up over a series of hills and passes until you reach the house, set on its own private hill-ridge, 700 m above sea level. The views are wonderful.

Le Silve is an old farmhouse (parts of it very old indeed – 10th century) converted to its new purpose with great sympathy and charm. There is a delightfully rambling feel to the place, with rooms on a variety of levels. The rustic nature of the building is preserved perfectly – all polished tile floors, stone or white walls, beamed ceilings, the occasional rug – and it is furnished with country antiques. Public rooms are large and airy, bedrooms stylishly simple. The self-contained suites are in villas about 1.5 km from the main house.

We have had conflicting reports of the food, which uses produce from the associated farm. Recently, a reader praised the 'very modern Italian cooking' (also pointing out that portions were small) while a previous guest complained about the 'pretentious *cuisine minceur* at astronomical prices'. What do you think? Le Silve is close enough to Assisi for sightseeing expeditions but remote enough for complete seclusion – and with good sports facilities immediately on hand (fair-sized pool). But it's not for vertigo sufferers.
~

NEARBY sights of Assisi.
LOCATION in countryside 12 km E of Assisi, between S444 and S3 (ask hotel for directions); ample car parking
FOOD breakfast, lunch, dinner; room service
PRICE €€€
ROOMS 11 double, 3 single, 4 self-contained suites, all with bath; all rooms have phone, TV, minibar, safe
FACILITIES 2 sitting rooms, dining room, bar, terrace, swimming pool, tennis, sauna, riding, archery, mini-golf, motorbike **CREDIT CARDS** AE, DC, V
DISABLED not suitable **CLOSED** mid Nov-mid Jan **MANAGER** Daniela Taddia

PERUGIA

BEVAGNA

L'ORTO DEGLI ANGELI
~ TOWN HOTEL ~

Via Dante Alighieri, 06031 Bevagna, Perugia
TEL (0742) 360130 **FAX** (0742) 361756
E-MAIL ortoangeli@ortoangeli.it **WEBSITE** www.ortoangeli.it

BEVAGNA IS ANOTHER OF THOSE SLEEPY little Umbrian places full of artistic gems, this time on the old Via Flaminia. Situated in the centre of town, l'Orto degli Angeli is a 17thC property which is remarkable for two features. The delightful hanging garden occupies the site of a Roman amphitheatre, and one rough stone wall of the pretty, lemon-painted restaurant is a remnant of a first century temple to Minerva.

The grandly-named Antonini Angeli Nieri Mongalli family have restored their fascinating home with much care. Its dimensions are grand, too, complete with frescoes, aged terracotta floors and vast stone fireplaces, but it manages to be homely and comfortable too – anything but overwhelming. The bedrooms are imaginatively decorated with great style; smart fabrics blend with the original terracotta floor tiles, gorgeous family antiques and painted woodwork. Modern equipment is carefully hidden from view. Four big rooms have been added in a converted wing of the house across the garden, and these are more modern, done out in a contemporary country rustic style with smart modern bathrooms.

The restaurant occupies an amazing space in what was once the ambulatory of a Roman amphitheatre. Eating in this barrel vaulted room, with the brick arches of the amphitheatre visible in the stone walls, is truly extraordinary. The food is fantastic too (jams and cakes are home made).

~

NEARBY Assisi (24 km); Perugia (45 km); Spello (13 km).
LOCATION 8 km SW of Foligno, in centre of town; public car parking 100 m
FOOD breafast, lunch, dinner
PRICE €€€
ROOMS 9 double and 9 suites, 7 with bath, 7 with shower; all rooms have phone, TV, air conditioning, minibar, safe, hairdrier
FACILITIES breakfast room, restaurant, sitting room, reading room, garden
CREDIT CARDS AE, DC, MC, V **DISABLED** not suitable **CLOSED** mid Jan-mid Feb
PROPRIETORS Tiziana and Francesco Antonini Angeli Nieri Mongalli

PERUGIA

BOVARA DI TREVI

CASA GIULIA
~ COUNTRY VILLA ~

Via Corciano 1, Bovara di Trevi, 06039 Perugia
TEL (0742) 78257 **FAX** (0742) 381632
E-MAIL casagiulia@umbria.net **WEBSITE** www.casagiulia.com

CASA GIULIA, parts of which go back to the 14thC, is both an excellent base for touring Umbria's famous cities (Assisi, Perugia, Spoleto and Todi are all within easy driving distance) and a great place in which to relax from the rigours of cultural tourism. Convenient for the main Spoleto-Perugia highway, but in no way disturbed by traffic, the villa has a withdrawn character as though time stopped still here sometime in the 1930s. The principal sitting room (open only on request), is a long rectangular area with doors and windows opening on to the garden, and is full of bric-a-brac collected by the owner's grandparents: *objets d'art*, old toys and cameras displayed in a glass-fronted bookcase, a collection of antique walking sticks and umbrellas.

In the rest of the house a solid, bourgeois atmosphere reigns. The breakfast room is elegant and uncluttered, with a black-and-white marble tiled floor (in summer breakfast is served under a pergola, just in front of the house). Bedrooms are a touch spartan, perhaps because some of them are located in the old servants' quarters – more a question of atmosphere than comfort.

~

NEARBY Assisi (22 km); Perugia (50 km); Spoleto (12 km).
LOCATION in its own grounds just outside village of Bovara, near Trevi; own car parking
FOOD breakfast
PRICE €
ROOMS 7 doubles: 5 with own bath or shower; 2 sharing one bathroom; 2 mini-apartments for 3 people (min. stay 3 days) with kitchenettes
FACILITIES sitting room, breakfast room, garden, swimming pool, meeting room
CREDIT CARDS accepted
DISABLED one suitable room **PETS** please check first
CLOSED never **LANGUAGES** French, some English
PROPRIETOR Caterina Alessandrini Petrucci

PERUGIA

CAMPELLO SUL CLITUNNO

IL VECCHIO MOLINO
∾ OLD MILL ∾

Pissignano, Via del Tempio 34, 06042 Perugia
TEL (0743) 521122 **FAX** (0743) 275097
E-MAIL info@ilvecchiomolino.it **WEBSITE** www.perugiaonline.com

IT IS A MYSTERY how this inn, so close to the busy Perugia-Spoleto road, remains such an oasis of tranquillity. Almost the only sound is of gurgling brooks winding through the leafy gardens. As befits an old mill, all the buildings live in close harmony with the river: the drive sweeps around the mill pond to a creeper-covered building against which big old grinding-stones rest. The gardens are a spit of land, with weeping willows dipping into streams on both sides. Water even runs through some of the old working parts, where the mill machinery has been built into the decorative scheme.

There seems to be no end to the number of public rooms, all furnished in a highly individual manner: elegant white couches in front of a big brick fireplace, surmounted by carved wooden lamps; tables with lecterns bearing early editions of Dante's Purgatorio; mill wheels used as doors. The bedrooms were, we were relieved to note, pleasingly dry and decorated in a restrained manner with fine antiques, the white walls lit up by parchment-shaded lamps.

Remember that the hotel is popular in the wedding season and during the Spoleto festival.

∾

NEARBY Spoleto (11 km); Perugia (50 km).
LOCATION 50 km SE of Perugia between Trevi and Spoleto; in its own grounds by the Clitunno river; ample car parking
FOOD breakfast
PRICE €-€€
ROOMS 2 single, 6 double, 5 suites, all with bath or shower, phone, minibar; some with air conditioning
FACILITIES sitting rooms, bar, gardens
CREDIT CARDS AE, DC, MC, V
DISABLED access difficult **PETS** small dogs accepted
CLOSED Nov-Mar **LANGUAGES** English, French, German
PROPRIETOR Paolo Rapanelli

PERUGIA

CASALINI

LA ROSA CANINA
~ FARM GUESTHOUSE ~

Via dei Mandorli 23, Casalini, Panicale, 06064 Perugia
TEL & FAX (075) 8350660
E-MAIL info@larosacanina.it **WEBSITE** www.larosacanina.it

A LONG AND WINDING TRACK takes you out of the village of Casalini for almost 3 km before you reach the hushed, olive-flanked valley where La Rosa Canina lies. Sandro Belardinelli and his wife made their home here in 1989, setting aside part of two 15thC cottages as guest quarters.

The dog-rose, from which the farm takes its name, is just one of the profusion of flowers which give the banks of the front garden their perennial colour. Behind the house, the menagerie of animals and the wire-fenced vegetable garden breathe real country living into what might have been just another converted farmhouse.

Inside, the guest rooms are reasonably proportioned and furnished with a hotch-potch of furniture, old and not so old. The wooden mangers in the downstairs dining room are a reminder that it was once a cattle stall. The dinner menu, based upon traditional cucina umbra, varies according to season, but Swiss-born Signora Belardinelli places emphasis on the quality of her food – all vegetables are home produce, as is the olive oil, much of the meat, and the jam on the breakfast table

~

NEARBY Lake Trasimeno (8 km); Panicale (8 km).
LOCATION 3 km along a track, above the village of Casalini; ample car parking
FOOD breakfast and dinner
PRICE B&B €; minimum stay 3 nights
ROOMS 5 double and 3 triple rooms, all with bath; all rooms centrally heated.
FACILITIES restaurant; garden, swimming pool, riding (lessons also available), archery, table tennis, bowls
CREDIT CARDS AE, MC, V
DISABLED no special facilities
PETS not accepted
CLOSED Nov-Easter.
LANGUAGES German, some English
PROPRIETOR Sandro Belardinelli

PERUGIA

CASTEL RIGONE

RELAIS LA FATTORIA
~ TOWN HOTEL ~

Via Rigone 1, Castel Rigone, Lago Trasimeno, 06060 Perugia
TEL (075) 845322 **FAX** (075) 845197
E-MAIL pammelati@edisons.it **WEBSITE** www.relaislafattoria.com

O**N THE HILLS** behind Lake Trasimeno lies the small medieval town of Castel Rigone, a mere handful of houses grouped about a handsome piazza, and right at its centre is this pleasant, family-run hotel occupying what was once a manor house.

You feel a sense of welcome the moment you step inside the reception, with its wooden ceiling, stone walls and comfortable Knole sofas; keen young staff are on hand. The public rooms are tastefully decorated, with Persian rugs on the polished cork floors and bright modern paintings on the white walls. The only addition to the building that has been allowed by the Italian Fine Arts Ministry is a restaurant perfectly in keeping with the original style. Dishes include fresh fish from the lake. Bed-rooms have been designed with an eye more to modern comfort than to individual style and some have lake views. The bathrooms are bright and new.

Along the entire front of the house is a terrace with sitting areas and a small swimming-pool. An extensive buffet breakfast (home-made bread and jams, cheeses and cured meats) is served here in fine weather.

~

NEARBY Perugia (27 km); Assisi (35 km); Gubbio (50 km).
LOCATION 27 km NW of Perugia, in centre of town; car parking nearby
FOOD breakfast, lunch, dinner
PRICE €-€€€€
ROOMS 3 single, 23 double, 3 junior suites, all with bath or shower (suites with Jacuzzis), phone, TV, minibar
FACILITIES sitting room, restaurant, terrace/garden, swimming pool
CREDIT CARDS AE, DC, MC, V
DISABLED no special facilities
PETS check first **CLOSED** never; restaurant only, Jan
LANGUAGES English, French, German
PROPRIETORS Pammelati family

PERUGIA

CASTEL RITALDI

LA GIOIA
~ COUNTRY HOUSE HOTEL ~

Cole del Marchese 60, 06044 Castel Ritaldi, Perugia
TEL (0743) 254068 **FAX** (0743) 254046
E-MAIL benvenuti@lagioia.biz **WEBSITE** www.lagioia.biz

HAVING RUN HER OWN interior decorating business in Zurich, Marianne Aerni-Kühne was in an ideal position to restore this 300-year-old oil and grain mill and, indeed, she and her husband Daniel have done a beautiful job. La Gioia is situated in an utterly peaceful position at the bottom of a wide valley, near several of Umbria's bigger towns, but also within easy reach of such undiscovered gems as Bevagna and Montefalco. The pale stone building stands in its own extensive grounds, which include an attractive pool, lawns, terraces and plenty of chairs to lounge on while listening to the birdsong under the shade of big white umbrellas. Inside, typical rustic features (*cotto* floors, beamed ceilings, exposed brickwork and so on) have been tastefully enhanced by the use of earthy, Mediterranean colours - the design aesthetic is a combination of Tuscan and northern European. The living room is welcoming; full of comfortable chairs and sofas, and the shelves are stacked with books, newspapers and music.

The bedrooms have been individually decorated with much attention to detail: underfloor heating and duvets on the beds make them very cosy in cooler weather. Some are split level with either a bed or sitting area on the top level, while others have a private terrace overlooking the garden. At La Gioia, food and wine are considered to be an important part of your stay (the chef uses home-grown or local produce), and half board is encouraged, especially during high season.

~

NEARBY Assisi (35km); Spoleto (13km); Todi (35km); Terni (45km).
LOCATION 13 km NW of Spoleto; in ample grounds; car parking
FOOD breakfast, dinner; light lunch on request
PRICE €€; €€€ half board
ROOMS 11 double, all with bath or shower, several with private garden; all rooms have phone, TV, safe, hairdrier
FACILITIES bar, sitting room, library, restaurant, terraces, garden, swimming pool
CREDIT CARDS MC, V **DISABLED** adapted rooms **PETS** accepted **CLOSED** Nov, Jan-Feb
PROPRIETORS Marianne and Daniel Aerni-Kühne

PERUGIA

CENERENTE

CASTELLO DELL'OSCANO
~ CONVERTED CASTLE ~

Cenerente, 06134 Perugia
TEL (075) 690 125 **FAX** (075) 690 666
E-MAIL info@oscano.com **WEBSITE** www.oscano.it

AT FIRST SIGHT Castello dell'Oscáno appears like a fairytale medieval castle: ivy-clad turrets, battlements and crenellated towers rise above a steep, hillside pine forest. In fact, this is an 18thC re-creation, and the inside reveals the 18thC's genius for civilized living.

The interiors are finely proportioned, spacious and light. The hall rises the entire height of the castle, with an imposing carved stairway, polished wood floors and neo-Gothic windows. One public room leads into another, all filled with the castle's original furniture: a library which will entrance any bibliophile with its carved Classical book-cases and 18thC volumes; sitting rooms with wooden panelling, tapestries and sculpted fireplaces; a dining room with old display cases full of Deruta pottery.

Upstairs, the floors are of geometrically patterned, black-and-white marble. There are only ten bedrooms in the castle, each with its own antique furnishing. The remainder, in the Villa Ada next door, are less exciting and cheaper. The most spectacular (but strictly for the agile) is in the turret, with a four-poster bed and a door to the ramparts which look over the romantic gardens below.

~

NEARBY Perugia (5 km); Assisi (28 km); Gubbio (40 km).
LOCATION on a hillside in its own grounds; ample car parking
FOOD breakfast, dinner
PRICE €€€€ (Castello)–€€ (VIlla Ada)
ROOMS 11 double (Castello), 8 double, 2 single (Villa Ada); all with bath or shower, phone, TV, minibar, air conditioning
FACILITIES bar, gardens, swimming pool
CREDIT CARDS AE, DC, MC, V
DISABLED 1 suitable bedroom
PETS accepted
CLOSED never; restaurant only, 15 Jan -15 Feb
LANGUAGES English, French
MANAGER Maurizio Bussolati

PERUGIA

CITTA DELLA PIEVE

HOTEL VANNUCCI
~ TOWN HOTEL ~

Via I. Vanni 1, 06062 Città della Pieve, Perugia
TEL (0578) 298063 **FAX** (0578) 297954
E-MAIL info@hotel-vannucci.com **WEBSITE** www.hotel-vannucci.com

PROPERTY DEVELOPER and interior designer Alison Deighton has owned a holiday home in delightful Città della Pieve for years, so when the venerable old Hotel Vannucci came up for sale, she was in a good position to take on the project of breathing new life into the place.

The square, grey-shuttered building is set in a pretty garden a stone's throw from the centre of the town. Inside, while the design makes use of local materials and techniques and the contemporary furniture is based on traditional styles, the result is refreshingly different. The reception area is dominated by an imposing staircase in pale, varnished wood, and some amazing light fittings. On the left is an inviting sitting room with an open fireplace and on the right, the open-plan bar area. Upstairs, the bedrooms vary in terms of shape and size, but are all done out along the same clean cut, modern lines; design details include custom-made carved bedheads from Bali and lamps from Turkey.

Food is important at the Vannucci and there are two restaurants. One serves casual, bistro-style food and pizzas, while at elegant Zafferano you can sample the chef's excellent creative takes on local dishes.

~

NEARBY Cathedral; Orvieto (40 km); Lake Trasimeno (20 km).
LOCATION In centre of town; public car parking nearby
FOOD breakfast, lunch, dinner
PRICE €
ROOMS 2 singles, 28 double and twin, all with bath or shower; all rooms have phone, TV, air conditioning, minibar, hairdrier, safe
FACILITIES sitting rooms, bar, 2 restaurants, lift, gym, sauna, Jacuzzi, terrace, garden
CREDIT CARDS AE, DC, MC, V **DISABLED** adapted rooms
PETS accepted **CLOSED** mid Jan-late Feb
PROPRIETOR Alison Deighton

PERUGIA

GUBBIO

VILLA MONTEGRANELLI
~ COUNTRY VILLA ~

Monteluiano, Gubbio, 06024 Perugia
TEL (075) 9220185 **FAX** (075) 9273372
E-MAIL villa.montegranelli@tin.it **WEBSITE** www.villamontegranellihotel.it

THE FACT THAT THIS 18thC villa is based on an original fortified building of the 13thC helps to explain the unadorned severity of the exterior. Massive and square, built of hewn stone, it stands in its own park surrounded by pines and centuries-old cypresses. From the gardens there is a view over to the light-grey stone city hanging on to the mountainside (a view that unfortunately includes the cement factory that has been allowed next to this dignified town).

In stark contrast, most of the interiors are in a light 18thC style: airily spacious public rooms with ornate plasterwork, frescoes and elaborate marble door surrounds, probably more suitable for the numerous weddings and official functions that take place here than for sitting and relaxing. The bedrooms are much more simply done (except for the main suite) and some are quite small. They all have excellent bathrooms.

The breakfast and dining rooms are in the lower, 13thC, part of the villa, with thick stone walls, vaulted ceilings and old brick arches. It is renowned for its restaurant, and you will appreciate the sophisticated cuisine and attentive service.

~

NEARBY Gubbio (5 km); Perugia (38 km); Assisi (35 km).
LOCATION 5 km SW of Gubbio, in its own grounds; ample car parking
FOOD breakfast, lunch, dinner
PRICE €€-€€€
ROOMS 20 double, 1 single, all with bath or shower, phone, TV, minibar
FACILITIES sitting rooms, restaurant, gardens
CREDIT CARDS AE, DC, MC, V **DISABLED** no special facilities
PETS dogs accepted
CLOSED never
LANGUAGES English, French, German
PROPRIETOR Salvatore Mongelli

PERUGIA

MONTECASTELLO VIBIO

FATTORIA DI VIBIO
~ FARM GUESTHOUSE ~

Buchella 1a, 9-Doglio, Montescastello Vibio, 05010 Perugia
TEL (075) 8749607 **FAX** (075) 8780014
E-MAIL info@fattoriadivibio.com **WEBSITE** www.fattoriadivibio.com

O CCASIONALLY, the whole atmosphere of a place is captured by a small detail: here it is the hand-painted pottery used to serve the delicious meals which reveals the relaxed elegance of this renovated 18thC farmhouse. The style is modern rustic Italian, with pleasing open spaces, defined by white walls that contrast with the colourful fabrics and ceramics. Light, airy and well-proportioned, there is an air of effortless simplicity which, you quickly realize, required a great deal of taste and effort. Most of the bedrooms, of similar style, are in the house next door. In recent years the place has been developed, but still retains its charm.

The Saladini family are serious about their visitors' comforts and wellbeing. Much of what is offered in the dining room comes out of the farm or the market garden and the preparation is a spectacle in itself, open to all. The menu changes daily. If you need to lose calories you can swim, play table-tennis, ride or walk in the magnificent countryside around; there is also a tennis court nearby. Or you may prefer to relax in the beautifully kept gardens, or in the outdoor pool and massage area that overlook the national park below, or even in the heated infinity pool with its glass wall that gives on to the same amazing view. This soothing guesthouse is great value for money - look out for their special offers.

~

NEARBY Todi (20 km); Orvieto (30 km).
LOCATION on quiet hillside off S448 road between Todi and Orvieto; car parking
FOOD breakfast, lunch, dinner
PRICE €€-€€ (half-board); one week minimum stay in August
ROOMS 14 double and 4 self-catering cottages, all with bath or shower; TV
FACILITIES sitting room, dining room and terrace, outdoor bar in summer garden, swimming pool, bikes, horse riding, fishing
CREDIT CARDS AE, DC, MC, V **DISABLED** one suitable room **PETS** small dogs
CLOSED mid Jan-mid Feb **LANGUAGES** French, little English
PROPRIETORS Gabriella, Giuseppe & Filippo Saladini

PERUGIA

MONTEFALCO

VILLA PAMBUFFETTI
~ VILLA HOTEL ~

Via della Vittoria 20, Montefalco, 06036 Perugia
TEL (0742) 379417, 378823 **FAX** (0742) 379245
E-MAIL info@villapambufetti.it **WEBSITE** www.villapambufetti.it

LIKE HEMINGWAY IN SPAIN, the poet D'Annunzio seems to have stayed everywhere in Italy; however, in the case of Villa Pambuffetti the claim is better justified than most. Not only did he dedicate a poem to the nearby walled town of Montefalco (known as 'Um-bria's balcony' for its unrivalled views of the region, but the villa itself has a turn-of-the-century elegance that fits the poet's legend.

Ten thousand square metres of shady garden surround the main building. Inside, furniture and decoration have been kept almost as they were at the start of the 1900s when the Pambuffetti family began taking 'paying guests': floors and panelling of seasoned oak, bamboo armchairs (which took D'Annunzio's fancy), Tiffany lampshades and old family photographs in art nouveau frames pay tribute to a century that started optimistically. Many of the bedrooms are furnished with the family's older and finer antiques and all have bathrooms which, though recent, are, stylistically, nearly perfect. If you like a room with a view, try the tower, which has one of the six-windowed, all-round variety. The dining room's view is more modest, but then the food deserves attention, too.

~

NEARBY Montefalco, Assisi (30 km); Perugia (46 km).
LOCATION just outside Montefalco, in its own grounds; ample car parking
FOOD breakfast, dinner
PRICE €€€-€€€€
ROOMS 11 double; 1 single; 3 suites; 2 with bath, the rest with shower, TV, minibar, air conditioning
FACILITIES sitting room, bar restaurant, loggia, garden, swimming pool
CREDIT CARDS AE, DC, MC, V
DISABLED 2 rooms on ground floor **PETS** not accepted
CLOSED never
LANGUAGES English, French, German, Spanish
MANAGERS Mauro and Alessandra Pambuffetti

PERUGIA

VILLA DI MONTESOLARE
~ COUNTRY VILLA HOTEL ~

Colle San Paolo, Panicale, 06070 Perugia
TEL (075) 832376 **FAX** (075) 8355462
E-MAIL info@villamontesolare.it **WEBSITE** www.villamontesolare.it

HIGH WALLS KEEP OUT the arid scenery around, enclosing the stuccoed villa in a green oasis. The present building dates back to 1780, although the 16thC chapel in the garden suggests a much earlier house was on the site. When the present owners bought it, they set about restoring the 19thC garden (and the secret garden behind it), building the swimming pool a discreet distance away, and converting the villa without interfering with its patrician character.

The result is one of the most comfortable country retreats of the Trasimeno area. The bedrooms of the villa retain their original character – beamed ceilings, quarry tile floors and whitewashed walls, furnished in squirely fashion with turn-of-the-century high-backed beds, cabinets and wardrobes. The cool blue sitting room on the piano nobile certainly is noble, while the dining rooms and the bar are situated more humbly, downstairs In 1995, Mrs Strunk and her husband Filippo converted a casa colonica which stands outside the walls. They divided it into five suites, building by it the villa's second swimming pool. Another annexe has also been added recently. Rooms are simply furnished in country style.

~

NEARBY Panicale (12 km); Città della Pieve (25 km).
LOCATION 2 km N of the SS 220, direction Colle S. Paolo; ample car parking
FOOD breakfast, lunch and dinner
PRICE €€€-€€€€
ROOMS 13 double; 10 superior rooms, 7 suites, all with bathroom; all rooms have air conditioning
FACILITIES 2 dining rooms, bar, sitting room; 2 swimming pools, tennis court, conference centre, cooking classes, wine tasting, classical music concert
CREDIT CARDS DC, MC, V
DISABLED 1 suitable apartment **PETS** if small, well-behaved **CLOSED** never
LANGUAGES English, German, French
PROPRIETOR Rosemarie Strunk and Filippo Iannarone

PERUGIA

PONTE PATTOLI

IL COVONE
~ COUNTRY VILLA GUESTHOUSE ~

Strada della Fratticiola 2, Ponte Pattoli, 06080 Perugia
TEL (075) 694140 **FAX** (075) 694140
E-MAIL info@covone.com **WEBSITE** www.italiaabc.com

PARTS OF VILLA IL COVONE date back to medieval times – the tower was once used to watch over the nearby Tiber. Today, the visitor is more conscious of the 18thC additions and the romantically peeling 19thC façade, which gives it the air of a classic Italianate villa.

The main hall, once an open courtyard, now glassed over, and the downstairs sitting rooms hold the family accretions of several centuries – portraits hanging higgledy-piggledy on cracking plaster remind you that this is still the Taticchi family's home. Upstairs, the guest quarters comprise bedrooms of different shapes and sizes, each spacious and high-ceilinged. The furniture has certainly seen better days (as has the house), but that is exactly what gives the place its charm. The eight rooms in the annex, across the way in the equestrian centre, are more modern, and perhaps more comfortable, but lack the fading splendour of the main house.

Dinner, shared with the family around one large table, includes Umbrian specialities such as *gnocchetti di ricotta* (small potato dumplings in a ricotta cheese sauce), pork roasted in the wood oven and *gelato in cialda* (ice cream in a nest of sponge).

~

NEARBY Perugia (10 km); Assisi (30 km).
LOCATION 2 km W of SS3-bis; gardens and private car parking
FOOD breakfast, lunch and evening meal
PRICE (€)
ROOMS 4 double rooms in villa, not all with private bathroom; 8 double rooms with shower, in annex
FACILITIES sitting room, dining room; billiards, table tennis; garden, horse riding (lessons available)
CREDIT CARDS AE, MC, V
DISABLED no facilities available **PETS** small animals only
CLOSED never **LANGUAGES** Some English
PROPRIETORS Cesare and Elena Taticchi

PERUGIA

SEMI DI MELA
~ FARMHOUSE HOTEL ~

Petroia 36, Scritto, Gubbio, 06020 Perugia
TEL & FAX (075) 920039
E-MAIL info@semidimela.com

A DIFFICULT TRACK takes you down, past the castle of Petroia, to this *casa colonica*, a farm worker's cottage restored over a decade ago and recently converted into three apartments, situated on a large rural estate. A downstairs beam shows that it was already standing in 1690, but its recent restoration has rather deprived it of that rough, rural character. The traditional oak and brick ceilings remain, but the smooth plasterwork and neat carpentry are all too perfect.

The bedrooms are comfortable, furnished simply in traditional rustic style. Every window opens on to awesome views of the Appennine mountains to the east of Gubbio.

Francesco Pellegrini grows organic food for the supper table on his ten acres of land, as well as olives and cereal crops, while Antonella tends the poultry which roam freely around the yard, and runs the kitchen. The emphasis of the evenings is that very Italian pursuit of stare insieme (getting together). Individual tables in the dining-room have recently been replaced with a single large one at which Antonella and Francesco eat with their guests. Their limited knowledge of English or other languages is made up for by the warmth of their hospitality.

NEARBY Gubbio (15 km); Perugia (25 km).
LOCATION 2 km E of the SS298 between Perugia and Gubbio
FOOD breakfast and dinner
PRICE For 2 people for 1 week €€€€€
ROOMS Two 2 bed appartments, one 4 bed, all with heating and bathrooms
FACILITIES sitting/dining room; terrace, garden, archery, mountain bikes, swimming pool (bring towel)
CREDIT CARDS not accepted
DISABLED no special facilities
PETS not accepted
CLOSED 6 Jan–early Mar **LANGUAGES** some English
PROPRIETORS Antonella Requale & Francesco Pellegrini

PERUGIA

SPOLETO

GATTAPONE
~ TOWN HOTEL ~

Via del Ponte 6, Spoleto, 06049 Perugia
TEL (0743) 223447 **FAX** (0743) 223448
E-MAIL info@hotelgattapone.it **WEBSITE** www.caribusiness.it/gattapone

THERE ARE TWO THINGS you can do in this hotel just outside Spoleto's centre. The most obvious is to gape at the unparalleled views of the 13thC Bridge of Towers spanning the Tessino Valley. The other is to enjoy the quaintness of its Sixties jet-set decoration, all wood, glass, chrome and leather. If you tire, as some do, of the rustic antique look, then you will enjoy the now dated, but meticulously maintained 'modern' style.

The hotel is a favourite of the Festival crowd, and the walls of the bar are festooned with pictures of the famous and would-be famous who throng its salons late into the evening. Even if you do not stay at the Gattapone, you will notice it. From the outside it looks like a solid, two-storey villa with classic ochre walls and green shutters. Inside, one notices how the original building and its more modern extension have been constructed downwards to exploit the hillside position. Many of the bedrooms have large picture windows to capture the panorama.

We visited the hotel in low season and enjoyed the peace and quiet. During the Festival (June-July), rooms are hard to get.

~

NEARBY Assisi 48 km; Todi 42 km; Perugia 63 km.
LOCATION on hillside, just outside historic centre of Spoleto; no special parking facilities
FOOD breakfast
PRICE €€€-€€€€€
ROOMS 7 double, 7 junior suites, all with bath or shower, phone, TV, minibar
FACILITIES breakfast room, sitting room, bar, terrace
CREDIT CARDS AE, DC, MC, V
DISABLED no special facilities
PETS accepted
CLOSED never
LANGUAGES English, French
PROPRIETOR Pier Giulio Hanke

PERUGIA

LA MACCHIA
~ COUNTRY HOTEL ~

Licina 11, Spoleto 06049 Perugia
TEL & FAX (0743) 49059
WEBSITE www.argoweb.it/hotel_lamacchia

SPOLETO, ONE OF THE MOST interesting of the southern Umbrian towns, is also one of the most congested, with a confusing one-way system and few places to park. From late June until mid-July, during Spoleto's world-famous Festival of Two Worlds, it is also notoriously difficult to find a room. This quiet hotel, tucked away in the fold of a hillside, yet close to the centre, is surrounded by olive groves with grazing donkeys, and offers a welcome alternative for those in search of a peaceful stay.

Carla and Claudio's hotel started life in the 1980s as a country osteria specializing in the local *cucina spoletana.* Today the restaurant is full of locals enjoying the simple (but good) food, in particular the delicious pizza. It was only recently that they opened their hotel, and the place is full of Claudio's 'antiques' - old TVs, radios and pots - adding character to what is basically a simple, modern building. A separate entrance spares guests from the occasional inconvenience caused by large dinners in the downstairs banqueting room. The style throughout is modern, though the old barn, now a shady portico, and the gnarled olive tree in the front court-yard, are a reminder of the building's original use. In each of the well-lit bedrooms, the chestnut furniture has been made by local craftsmen. Some beds have old wrought iron heads and splendidly firm bases.

~

NEARBY Spoleto (2 km); Fonti di Clitunno (10 km).
LOCATION 0.5 km from the old via Flaminia, just N of Spoleto; ample car parking
FOOD breakfast, lunch (Sun and holidays only), dinner
PRICE rooms € with breakfast
ROOMS 10 double, 1 single with shower, air conditioning, satellite television, minibar, central heating
FACILITIES sitting room/breakfast room, 2 dining rooms (one for residents the other for non) bar, restaurant, garden, swimming pool, bikes
CREDIT CARDS AE, DC, MC, V **DISABLED** 2 bedrooms **PETS** not accepted
CLOSED never; restaurant only, Tue **LANGUAGES** English
PROPRIETORS Carla Marini and Claudio Sabatini

PERUGIA

SPOLETO

SAN LUCA
~ TOWN HOTEL ~

Via Interna delle Mura 21, Spoleto 06049, Perugia
TEL (0743) 223399 **FAX** (0743) 223800

WHEN POPE INNOCENT II came to this spot in 1198, his holy presence is reputed to have caused a fountain miraculously to begin spouting clear and plentiful water, thus giving immediate relief and renewed strength to himself and his retinue. Today the site is occupied by an impressive 19thC building with soft yellow painted walls, wooden doors and shutters, and a red-tiled roof, which was transformed after extensive renovation into an elegant hotel in 1995. The yellow colour scheme continues inside in the light, sunny hallway and sitting areas, where comfortable armchairs, some upholstered in bright yellow, others, more modern, in black leather, blend stylishly with antique furniture, a display of china tureens and attractive arrangements of flowers and plants. Several of the pastel-toned bedrooms have a balcony or terrace; all of them are sound-proofed and have large bathrooms with telephones.

Right in the centre of Spoleto, but peacefully set in lush gardens, the San Luca also has a roof garden as well as a spacious internal courtyard, where it is still possible to sample the 'therapeutic' properties of the waters. We would welcome more reports.
~

NEARBY Assisi 48 km; Todi 42 km.
LOCATION in historic city centre; car parking
FOOD buffet breakfast
PRICE €€€-€€€€€
ROOMS 32 double, 3 single, 1 suite, all with bath (some with Jacuzzi), 5 with shower, phone, air conditioning, minibar, hairdrier, safe
FACILITIES 2 sitting rooms, breakfast room, conference room, 2 lifts, courtyard, garden, roof garden
CREDIT CARDS AE, DC, MC, V
DISABLED two adapted rooms **PETS** small dogs accepted
CLOSED never **LANGUAGES** English, German, French
PROPRIETOR Daniela Zuccari

PERUGIA

TORGIANO

LE TRE VASELLE
~ TOWN HOTEL ~

Via Garibaldi 48, Torgiano, 06089 Perugia
TEL (075) 9880447 **FAX** (075) 9880214
E-MAIL 3vaselle@3vaselle.it **WEBSITE** www.3vaselle.it

THREE MONASTIC WINE JUGS discovered during the restoration of the original 17thC *palazzo* are what give this exceptional hotel its name and its theme: wine. Owned by the Lungarotti family, makers of Umbria's finest vintages, the palazzo is packed with still lifes of grapes, prints of the gods carousing and statues of Bacchus. However, nothing but sober professionalism characterizes the day-to-day management.

Bedrooms, some in a more modern building behind the main one and others in a luxury annexe a short walk away, are all furnished to the highest standards: comfortable striped sofas, antique chests, individually chosen prints and lamps give an air of unrushed elegance. Public rooms are open and spacious, spanned by sweeping white arches and softly lit. Breakfast, an extensive buffet, is served on a secluded back terrace. The restaurant is outstanding, with a wine-list the size of a telephone directory.

A recent visitor to Le Tre Vaselle could report only improvements. It could not be more professional; you could not feel more at home.

~

NEARBY Deruta (5 km); Perugia (8 km); Assisi (16 km).
LOCATION in quiet street of village of Torgiano, 13 km SE of Perugia; car parking in nearby piazza
FOOD breakfast, lunch, dinner
PRICE €€€€-€€€€€
ROOMS 52 double, 2 singles, 7 suites; most with bath, some with shower; all rooms have central heating, air conditioning, phone, TV
FACILITIES sitting rooms, dining rooms, breakfast room, bar, terrace, swimming pool, sauna
CREDIT CARDS AE, DC, MC, V
DISABLED access possible
PETS not accepted
CLOSED never
LANGUAGES English, French, German
MANAGER Giovanni Margheritini

PERUGIA

TUORO SUL TRASIMENO

VILLA DI PIAZZANO
~ COUNTRY VILLA ~

Piazzano, 06069 Tuoro sul Trasimeno, Perugia
TEL (075) 826226 **FAX** (075) 826336
E-MAIL info@villadipiazzano.com **WEBSITE** www.villadipiazzano.com

APPROACHED VIA A LONG DRIVE lined with cypress trees, and situated in
gentle farmland on the Tuscan/Umbrian border, imposing Villa di
Piazzano was built by Cardinal Silvio Passerini in 1464 as a hunting lodge.
Note that in spite of the postal address, it is nearer Cortona than Tuoro.

When the Italo-Australian Wimpole family decided to settle here and
open a hotel after a lifetime of travel with the Australian diplomatic service, they found themselves with a major restoration job on their hands.

Today, the elegant, traditional decoration is very much in keeping with
the style of the house but allows for modern comforts. On the ground floor,
the public rooms include a welcoming salone with an open fire and a
pleasant, lemon-yellow-painted restaurant serving creative versions of
local dishes. At the top of the original sweeping stone staircase the spacious bedrooms are nicely furnished with a mix of antiques and reproduction pieces. One has a pretty painted ceiling. In front of the house is a terrace shaded by lime trees (where meals are served in summer) and a fine
Italianate garden below which lies a pool. The outlook is over fields and
the wooded hills where the Cardinal once hunted for boar.

~

NEARBY Cortona (6 kms); Trasimeno (16 kms); Perugia (40 kms).
LOCATION 6 kms south east of Cortona off the SP 35; drive through Pergo and
follow the signs. In open countryside; ample car parking
FOOD breakfast, light lunch, dinner
PRICE €€€
ROOMS 17 double and twin, all with bath or shower; all rooms have phone, TV,
minibar, air conditioning, hairdrier
FACILITIES sitting rooms, bar, restaurant, lift, pool, garden, terraces, mountain bikes
for hire
CREDIT CARDS AE, DC, MC, V **DISABLED** no special facilities
PETS small, well-behaved dogs accepted **CLOSED** mid Nov-early March
PROPRIETORS The Wimpole family

PERUGIA

BORGO SAN BIAGIO
~ SELF-CATERING HAMLET ~

Bookings only through CV Travel in the U.K.
TEL (0044) 02073845850 **FAX** (0044) 02073845899
E-MAIL italy@cvtravel.co.uk **WEBSITE** www.cvtravel.co.uk

A T NOON AND 6 PM the chapel bell tolls, as it has for hundreds of years, over this isolated hamlet on top of an Umbrian hill. Once a medieval community, now it consists of seven dwellings, rescued from ruin and individually equipped, plus a communal living/dining area and a large communal living area/games room in the old chapel. It's one of the most enchanting self-catering operations we've seen in Italy. We're reluctant to include such places unless they offer a certain level of service; here, not only the bell is rung, but the beds are changed (with cotton sheets) and dinner will be cooked each night if you want. The owner, friendly Renato Rondina, began restoring it in the early 1990s, bringing it off with skill and high standards: comfortable beds, cooking facilities and CD players in each dwelling. It's ideal for a group to rent together because taking just one of the houses, and having to rub along with unknown neighbours, might spoil the very special intimacy and peace. There's a great sense of timelessness, space, views to keep you musing for hours and an extra-long swimming pool. Crowning all is a 1,000-year-old, remarkably restored tower, sleeping two. The photo was taken from its roof, on which is a second (miniature) swimming pool.

~

NEARBY Cortona, Umbertide, Sansepolcro, Monterchi.
LOCATION very isolated, on hill top in own grounds – directions essential, supplied on booking
FOOD self-catering, but dinner by arrangement; real pizza oven
PRICE middle-range self-catering
ROOMS 7 self-catering dwellings, sleeping 2-4, all with en suite showers, living rooms, central heating, some with phone
FACILITIES games room, garden, swimming pool
CREDIT CARDS prepayment required, AE, MC, V accepted
DISABLED unsuitable **PETS** not accepted
CLOSED never **LANGUAGES** English
PROPRIETOR Renato Rondina

PERUGIA

ASSISI

HOTEL ALEXANDER

TOWN HOTEL

Piazza Chiesa Nuova 6, Assisi,
06081 Perugia

TEL (075) 816190
FAX (075) 816804
E-MAIL hpriori@umbriatravel.com
FOOD breakfast facilities
PRICE € **CLOSED** never

THIS SMALL FAMILY-RUN hotel is tucked away just off the central Piazza del Comune, and offers a useful alternative to Assisi's pricier central hotels. Its moderate-sized bedrooms have beamed ceilings and reproduction rustic furniture. Breakfast is served in the rooms. The Alexander has been renovated and extended in recent years, which has added to its attractions. A recent visitor describes it as 'nice, quiet and clean'; another rates it 'a lovely little hotel… staff helpful and friendly.'

ASSISI

COUNTRY HOUSE

COUNTRY GUESTHOUSE

San Pietro Campagna 178,
Assisi, 06081 Perugia

TEL & **FAX** (075) 816363
E-MAIL none
FOOD breakfast
PRICE €-€€ with breakfast
CLOSED never

THIS DELIGHTFUL STONE-BUILT guesthouse, just below the walls of Assisi, combines proximity with rural tranquility. Signora Silvana furnishes the comfortable bedrooms from the stock of the antiques business which she runs downstairs (18th and 19th century Umbrian furniture such as chests, tables, armchairs mirrors and beds). In summer you can swim in the pool and enjoy breakfast on the large terrace overlooking Santa Maria degli Angel, and in winter you can curl up by the fire with a book. Bedrooms, recently remodeled, are cool and large. Several guests have reported only positive things about their stay at the Country House, including finding Signora Ciammarughi friendly and helpful; one or two have been put off by her temperamental manner.

PERUGIA

ASSISI

UMBRA
TOWN HOTEL

*Via degli Archi 6, Assisi, 06081
Perugia*

TEL (075) 812240
FAX (075) 813653
E-MAIL
humbra@mail.caribusiness.it
FOOD breakfast, lunch, dinner
PRICE €€
CLOSED mid Jan-mid Mar

IN A CITY NOT NOTED for quality small hotels, the delightful family-run Umbra cannot be ignored. Tucked away down a little alley off the main square, it consists of several small houses, some dating back to the thirteenth century, each with a small gravelled courtyard garden shaded by a pergola. The interior is comfortable, in some parts more like a home than hotel. The bedrooms, most simply furnished, each has its own character. We enjoyed eating in the elegant dining room, but agreed with past reports that food was only 'all right'. (Plenty of alternative eating places nearby.) You can be sure of peace, and nothing is too much trouble for Alberto Laudenzi, whose family has run the hotel for more than 50 years.

ASSISI

VILLA GABBIANO
COUNTRY VILLA

Gabbiano, Assisi, 06081 Perugia

TEL & FAX (075) 8065278
E-MAIL
villagabbiano@villagabbiano.it
FOOD breakfast, dinner
PRICE €-€€
CLOSED never

THE 18thC COUNTRY VILLA of Assisi's ancient Fiumi-Sermattei family stands in their 150-acre olive estate and has been run as a guesthouse for more than a decade. Guests stay in the main villa or in one of the farmhouse apartments, all sympathetically restored. It is a working farm, which produces olive oil and breeds farmyard animals and saddle horses. Traditional Umbrian dishes are served in the great hall and include produce from the farm. There's a pool with a bar and a spectacular view in the tranquil, lime-shaded garden.

PERUGIA

MIRALAGO

FARM GUESTHOUSE

Piazza Mazzini 6, Castiglione del Lago, 06061 Perugia

TEL (075) 951157
FAX (075) 951924
E-MAIL none
FOOD restaurant and bar
PRICE €
CLOSED never

DESPITE A CENTRAL position on the main piazza, the quiet, spacious rear bedrooms have views over a corner of Lake Trasimeno. A useful stopover address but not for a longer stay. The bedrooms are nothing special. Despite the rather conventional reception hall with desk, the public areas are furnished in quite a pleasant, homely style. Most months, the downstairs restaurant, serving fish from the lakes as well as meatier, Umbrian dishes, spills on to the lake-view terrace. One recent visitor was very disappointed with his very plain bedroom, the cramped bathroom, and a 'dreadful' breakfast. Proprietors: Patrizi family. Reports welcome.

IL ROTOLONE

COUNTRY GUESTHOUSE

Sant'Anna, Gualdo Cattaneo, 06035 Perugia

TEL (0742) 91992
FAX (0742) 361307
E-MAIL none
FOOD breakfast, lunch, dinner
PRICE €
CLOSED never

THIS SMALL GUESTHOUSE, housed in old farm-workers' cottages on the Benincasa family estate, commands fine views out over wooded hills towards Assisi. The moderate-sized bedrooms are simply furnished in appropriate country style. The dinner menu makes imaginative use of the farm's organically grown vegetables. Gualdo Cattaneo is a 14th and 15thC hill town, historically much under the influence of Spoleto, and with an impressive fortified tower.

PERUGIA

ISOLA MAGGIORE

HOTEL DA SAURO

ISLAND HOTEL

Via Guglielmi 1, Isola Maggiore, 06060 Perugia

TEL (075) 826168
FAX (075) 825130
FOOD breakfast, lunch, dinner
PRICE € **CLOSED** 3 weeks in Nov
and mid-Jan to mid-Feb

A SHORT BOAT TRIP from Tuoro or Passignano takes you to Isola Maggiore, the second largest of the three Trasimeno islands, where St Francis of Assisi is said to have taken refuge on a stormy night in 1211. Although it stills looks like a 15thC fishing village, it is home to a renowned restaurant that also offers the island's only hotel accommodation. It is a modest, popular three-star, where the bedrooms are small, pine-furnished and somewhat characterless, but the Scarpocchi family's hospitality, the fish and pasta menus and the lake views more than compensate.

PERUGIA

BRUFANI

TOWN HOTEL

Piazza Italia 12, 06100 Perugia

TEL (075) 5732541
FAX (075) 5720210
E-MAIL
reservationsbru@sinahotels.it
WEBSITE www.brufanipalace.com
FOOD breakfast, lunch, dinner
PRICE €€€-€€€€
CLOSED never

I MPOSING FOYER with plush couches and copies of classical statues set in wall niches, this luxurious hotel has a coveted location inside the old town centre. Rooms are all sumptuously decorated: salons with painted ceilings and massive stone fireplaces, and bedrooms with antiques and rich fabrics. Unusually for a town hotel, some of the bedrooms have views of the Umbrian countryside, stretching to Assisi and Todi on the horizon. In the restaurant, 'Collins', which occupies a panoramic terrace in warm weather, the food is first-class with mainly Umbrian (many truffle-based) specialities. Refined atmosphere and high prices attract an up-market clientèle.

PERUGIA

LA CERQUA

FARM GUESTHOUSE

San Salvatore, Pietralunga, 06026
Perugia

TEL (075) 9460283
FAX (075) 9462033
E-MAIL info@cerqua.it
WEBSITE www.cerqua.it
FOOD breakfast, lunch, dinner
PRICE ©
CLOSED Jan -Feb

A N EXCELLENT BARGAIN for those who like the quiet rural life. Situated in panoramic northern Umbria between Citta di Castello and Gubbio and decorated in authentic rustic style, guests of La Cerqua can enjoy long walks in the oak forests between meals of hearty Umbrian fare. It is still a working organic farm, and the fruit from its trees goes to make the jam and liqueurs served in the guesthouse and for sale in the farm shop. The wood burned in the open fireplaces all comes from the farm's own forests. In addition to a small fishing lake nearby, there is horse riding, bikes for guests to use, and a lovely acorn-shaped swimming pool.

CASTELLO DI PETROIA

CASTLE

Petroia Scritto di Gubbio, 06020
Perugia

TEL (075) 920287
FAX (075) 920108
E-MAIL info@castellodipetroia.com
FOOD breakfast, dinner
PRICE ©-©©
CLOSED Jan-Mar

T HIS IS ABOUT as authentic as you can get: a 13thC castle, strategically located between Gubbio and Perugia overlooking the Chiascio valley, witness to many important events in the distant past, and hardly touched by time in the intervening years. There it sits, stark, romantic, isolated on its hilltop, offering just a few rooms to modern travellers, perhaps particularly to walkers, who are in retreat, for a few days at least, from modern life. Within the circle of castle walls stands a group of medieval buildings, with six rooms reserved for guests, each with private bath and sitting area, fridge, television and telephone. The castle's owners live there too, as their ancestors have done since the 15th century.

Perugia

Castello di Giomici

SELF-CATERING APARTMENTS

*Il Castello di Giomici, 06029
Valfabbrica, 06029 Perugia*

TEL (075) 901243
FAX (075) 901713 **E-MAIL**
reception@IlCastelloDiGiomici.it
FOOD none
PRICE € **CLOSED** never

THE 12TH C HAMLET which makes up Castello di Giomici tops a wooded hill above the peaceful valley of Valfabbrica. Much of the castle, impressive-looking with two towers and ramparts, has now been converted by Luciano Vagni into self-catering apartments, each furnished with smart rustic simplicity. The perfect place for energetic families, it has a large garden, swimming pool, bowls, table tennis, lake fishing and a games room. Unless you are in one of the self-catering apartments, you will need a car, as there are no nearby restaurants.

TERNI

BASCHI

LE CASETTE/POMURLO VECCHIO
∼ COUNTRY GUESTHOUSES ∼

Pomurlo Vecchio, Baschi, 05023 Terni
TEL (0744) 950190/950475 **FAX** (0744) 950500

Lazzaro Minghelli's 350-acre farm estate stretches from the southern shores of Lago di Corbara almost as far as Baschi. His romantic family home, Pomurlo Vecchio, is an eccentric 12thC tower, jutting out of a wooded hillock. It also has four small apartments, each with its separate entrance. They are homely, though rather frayed at the edges and in need of redecoration.

The principal guest accommodation, however, Le Casette, stands on the other side of the estate, towards Baschi. Its three stone cottages have been recently rebuilt around a central swimming pool on a hillside ridge. Though lacking the patina of age, they provide a summer oasis which is particularly suitable for families, Each room is simply decorated, with white plaster and exposed stone walls and comfortably furnished.

The restaurant, overseen by daughter Daniela, is noteworthy. Each course has a genuine farmhouse taste — 80 per cent of the ingredients are organically grown on the estate. This is complemented by the charm and warmth of the family, who eat with their guests and do everything to make them feel at home.

∼

NEARBY Orvieto (15 km); Todi (20 km).
LOCATION 1 km S of SS448 near Lago di Corbara; or 5 km E of Baschi towards Montecchio
FOOD breakfast, lunch, dinner
PRICE rooms €; DB&B €-€€ minimum stay one week in August
ROOMS 3 small apartments in main villa; 8 double rooms, 6 apartments in Le Casette complex (about 1 mile away); all with shower, refrigerator
FACILITIES central heating; restaurant, bar; swimming pool, horse riding
CREDIT CARDS none **DISABLED** 3 bedrooms
PETS by prior arrangement **CLOSED** never
LANGUAGES some English
PROPRIETORS Lazzaro and Daniela Minghelli

TERNI

BASCHI

LA PENISOLA
~ COUNTRY HOUSE AND RESTAURANT ~

Baschi, Strada per Todi (SS 448) 05023 Terni
TEL (0744) 950521 **FAX** (0744) 950524
E-MAIL info@penisola.net   **WEBSITE** www.penisola.net

UNDENIABLY MODERN, but stylish in its own way, La Penisola will appeal to travellers who enjoy contemporary comforts and the full range of facilities. Magnificently situated on the shores of Lago di Corbara, a man-made lake, the 'villa' was originally a set of 19thC farm buildings, but is now rigorously updated. The low-slung buildings, pleasantly rose-tinted, fit well into the tree-filled, undulating grounds that lead down to the lake. The interiors are defined by clean lines, occasionally broken by a traditional brick arch or fireplace. Furnishings are stylishly contemporary, and a minimalist approach to decoration gives a spacious feel.

The hotel certainly makes full use of its lakeside location: large picture windows carry your eyes over its rippling surface to the sloping green hills beyond. The gardens are meticulously cared for, with acres of rolling lawns and brightly coloured flowers in squat terracotta urns, and there is an outdoor pergola next to the restaurant where you can enjoy not just your meal and the view but also a cool evening breeze from the lake.

~

NEARBY Orvieto (10 km); Todi (15 km).
LOCATION lakeside location on SS 448 between Orvieto and Todi; own grounds; ample car parking
FOOD breakfast, lunch, dinner
PRICE €€
ROOMS 19 double, all with bath or shower, phone, TV, minibar
FACILITIES sitting room, bar, restaurant, garden, tennis court, swimming pool, five-a-side football, sauna
CREDIT CARDS AE, DC, MC, V
DISABLED 1 adapted room **PETS** check when booking
CLOSED never; restaurant only, Mon
LANGUAGES English, French, Spanish
MANAGER The Cramsts

TERNI

MONTELEONE D'ORVIETO

PALAZZO CONSOLI
~ VILLAGE GUESTHOUSE ~

Corso Vittorio Emanuele II 46, 05017 Monteleone d'Orvieto
TEL & FAX (0763) 834032
E-MAIL info@palazzoconsoli.it **WEBSITE** www.palazzoconsoli.it

WHEN STEPHEN AND ELISA Crowther (he English, she Italian) bought this 16thC *palazzo* situated in a charming, unspoilt hilltop village, it came complete with splendid antique furniture and pictures, as well as all sorts quirky personal possessions accumulated by the previous owner's grand-mother. The Crowthers have lovingly restored the house and added a cer-tain artistic flair of their own: the combination of grand *palazzo* with arty design details and the genuinely warm and enthusiastic welcome of the owners, for whom nothing is too much trouble, is genuinely captivating.

The five bedrooms (of varying sizes) are individually furnished and deco-rated in warm colours. Beds are made up with duvets and beautiful vin-tage linens, while other touches include fluffy coloured towels, fresh flow-ers, real hairdriers and trays with a bottle of local liqueur should guests care for a nightcap. The travertine marble bathrooms are super-modern. The comfortable sitting room has a TV and stereo and is well stocked with books and magazines, and there's a delightful, partially glassed-in veranda from where the far-reaching views are stunning. Breakfast is served in the *palazzo*'s original kitchen or in the tiny adjacent courtyard. Stephen is a real foodie and cooks for guests on request. As we went to press there were plans to open a restaurant.

~

NEARBY Orvieto (30 km); Citta della Pieve (7 km).
LOCATION In centre of hilltop village of Monteleone d'Orvieto; public car parking 50 metres
FOOD breakfast, dinner on request
PRICE €€
ROOMS 4 doubles and 1 twin, all with bath or shower; all rooms have hairdrier, minibar
FACILITIES breakfast room, sitting room, verandah
CREDIT CARDS MC, V **DISABLED** not suitable **PETS** not accepted
CLOSED 7 Jan-end Feb **PROPRIETORS** Elisa and Stephen Crowther

TERNI

NARNI

DEI PRIORI
~ TOWN HOTEL ~

Vicolo del Comune 4, Narni, 05035 Terni
TEL & FAX (0744) 726843
E-MAIL info@loggiadeipriori.it **WEBSITE** bellaumbria.net/hotel-Deipriori/home

TUCKED AWAY IN A QUIET ALLEY in the medieval heart of one of southern Umbria's unsung towns, this friendly small hotel provides an ideal staging post for travellers who prefer the 'backroads' route along the via Flaminia to Rome. As well as the magnificent Piazza dei Priori, the town's Romanesque duomo and the 14thC Palazzo del Podestà provide ample reason for an overnight detour.

The meat hooks in the bricked, vaulted ceiling of the entrance hall indicate that it was once the food store for the *palazzo*. Upstairs, the sitting rooms on the piano nobile, with their carved stone architraves, are altogether more worthy.

A lift, or a grandiose black oval staircase, takes you up to the comfortable modern bedrooms which look out into the central courtyard or over the pantiled roofs of the medieval borgo. A few have their own balconies.

Downstairs, the restaurant spills out into the courtyard in the summer months. Its menu is mainly Umbrian (the local pasta dish is manfricoli), although the Venetian chef adds the occasional northern dish.

~

NEARBY Ponte di Augusto (2 km); Otricoli (14 km).
LOCATION 20 m from the town's main Piazza dei Priori
FOOD breakfast, lunch, dinner
PRICE €
ROOMS 11 double, 5 single, 1 suite, all with shower; all rooms have, television, radio, minibar, central heating; 7 rooms with air conditioning
FACILITIES sitting room, breakfast room, bar, restaurant with tables also in the interior courtyard
CREDIT CARDS AE, DC, MC, V
DISABLED no facilities
PETS small well-behaved animals accepted
CLOSED never **LANGUAGES** some English
PROPRIETOR Maurizio Bravi

TERNI

ORVIETO

LA BADIA
~ OLD ABBEY ~

La Badia, Orvieto, 05019 Terni
TEL (07633) 01959 **FAX** (07633) 05396

ARRIVING AT TWILIGHT at La Badia is like landing in a scene from a Gothic novel: ruined arches, rooks cawing from a crenellated bell-tower, dark cypresses silhouetted against the sky and, across the valley, the evening profile of Orvieto's cathedral, secure on its fortress crag. But the golden stone monastery on the hill, surrounded by Umbria's intense green countryside, soon reveals itself as an outstanding hotel that would have delighted any Renaissance cardinal.

Restraint is the hallmark of this fine building's conversion into a distinctive hotel. The robust architecture of the old abbey is always allowed to speak for itself, and modern embellishments have been kept to a minimum. The heavy wooden period furniture goes well with the massive stone walls; wrought-iron lights illuminate vaulted ceilings; floors are either of plain or geometrically patterned terracotta. Here and there, an unexpectedly-placed church pew reminds the guest of what once was.

On the hill behind, is a pool fit for a pope. In front of the abbey, beside the famous 12-sided tower, is a peaceful garden where the meditative visitor can contemplate the view of Orvieto.

~

NEARBY Orvieto (5 km); Todi (40 km); Viterbo (45 km).
LOCATION on quiet hillside, 5 km S of Orvieto
FOOD breakfast, lunch, dinner
PRICE €€€-€€€€
ROOMS 3 single, 21 double, 7 suites; all with bath or shower; all rooms have phone, air conditioning, central heating
FACILITIES sitting room, breakfast room, bar, restaurant, conference room, tennis court, swimming pool
CREDIT CARDS AE, V
DISABLED access difficult **PETS** not allowed
CLOSED Jan and Feb **LANGUAGES** English
PROPRIETOR Luisa Fiume

TERNI

ORVIETO (CANALE)

FATTORIA LA CACCIATA
~ COUNTRY VILLA ~

La Cacciata 6, Orvieto, 05010 Terni
TEL (0763) 300892/305481 **FAX** (0763) 300892
WEBSITE www.argoweb.it/cacciata

IT IS A SHORT DRIVE up from the small village of Canale, through rows of vineyards, to Villa La Cacciata. Across the valley stands Orvieto's cathedral, seated majestically on its limestone pedestal; the villa's swimming-pool must surely have one of the top ten locations in all of Italy.

The main building, an aristocratic villa with a 19thC facelift, remains the home of *avvocato* Belcapo and his family, while four stone farm buildings around it have been converted into simple guest accommodation. Each bedroom retains the atmosphere of a farm cottage: beamed and tiled ceilings and terracotta floors with simple, somewhat spartan, furnishings. Most of them have idyllic pastoral views out over the estate. Bathrooms are shared, but this is more than reflected in the low charges.

The Belcapo family's estate produces one of the area's premier Orvieto Classico wines and fine olive oil.

The kitchen and restaurant in one of the buildings are periodically used for cookery courses. For the remainder of the time, the family offer a tempting menu of strictly Umbrian fare.

~

NEARBY Orvieto's cathedral and Pozzo di San Patrizio (4 km).
LOCATION Near the village of Canale, S of Orvieto
FOOD breakfast, dinner on request
PRICE ⓔ
ROOMS 11 double rooms, sharing 10 bathrooms, central heating
FACILITIES sitting room with television in each building, restaurant, bar; swimming pool, garden, riding
CREDIT CARDS none
DISABLED no facilities
PETS not accepted
CLOSED Christmas period
LANGUAGES some English
PROPRIETOR Settimio Belcapo

TERNI

ORVIETO

PALAZZO PICCOLOMINI
~ TOWN HOTEL ~

Piazza Ranieri 36, 05018 Orvieto, Terni
TEL (0763) 341743 **FAX** (0763) 391046
E-MAIL piccolomini.hotel@orvienet.it **WEBSITE** www.hotelpiccolomini.it

AT LAST A DECENT HOTEL has been created in the centre of this remarkable town which sits on a pedestal of tufa some 300 m above sea level. Orvieto is a charming place with a fabulous, candy-striped cathedral, an atmospheric *centro storico*, a choice of restaurants serving fine, regional food and last, but not least, an excellent local white wine.

Pale pink Palazzo Piccolomini (so-named after the family who built it at the end of the 16th century) is situated at the heart of the old city and was beautifully restored as a hotel in 1998. Inside, there is a wonderful sense of calm throughout the cool, vaulted rooms, which have been furnished with what some might call spartan good taste. In the spacious salon, wrought-iron candelabras and white covers on sofas and chairs are stylish against white walls and polished terracotta floors; filmy white curtains ripple in the breeze and filter the sunlight. The bedrooms, although varying in shape and size, are similar, with modern, dark wooden furniture and the odd splash of deep blue. Some have rooftop views. You eat breakfast in a vaulted basement room which has Etruscan origins.

~

NEARBY cathedral; underground caves.
LOCATION on the S side of town near Porta Romana; public car parking 200 m away
FOOD breakfast
PRICE ⓔⓔ
ROOMS 22 double and twin, 6 single, 3 suites, all with shower, all rooms have phone, TV, air conditioning, minibar, hairdrier
FACILITIES breakfast room, sitting room, bar, lift
CREDIT CARDS AE, DC, MC, V
DISABLED some adapted rooms
PETS accepted
CLOSED 1 week Jan
MANAGER Liliana Achilli

TERNI

ORVIETO

VILLA CICONIA
~ COUNTRY VILLA ~

Ciconia, Via dei Tigli 69, Orvieto, 05018 Terni
TEL (0763) 305582/3 **FAX** (0763) 302077
E-MAIL villaciconia@libero.it **WEBSITE** www.hotelvillaciconia.com

PROTECTED FROM THE NEARBY busy road and the encroachments of Orvieto's new suburbs by its tree-filled gardens, La Ciconia is a small, attractive 16thC grey stone villa with two bays of windows flanking an arched entrance. Inside, one encounters a variety of styles, such as spacious ground floor public rooms with geometric, polychrome tiled floors, massive stone fireplaces and frescoed friezes.

The bedrooms are in a more rustic style, with wrought iron or four-poster beds and antique chests that combine well with the exposed roof-beams and warm, terracotta floors. Bathrooms are spanking new and most have a shower rather than a bath.

The gardens are a delight, bounded by two streams. There is, unfortunately, some noise from the road outside. The restaurant serves Umbrian specialities with oil and wine from the owner's farms - popular for weddings, so it may get busy at weekends.

A pleasant alternative to La Badia (page 193) if the latter is full or you find it too expensive.

~

NEARBY Orvieto (3 km); Todi (33 km); Perugia (78 km).
LOCATION just outside Orvieto in its own grounds; ample car parking
FOOD breakfast, lunch, dinner
PRICE €€€-€€€€
ROOMS 12 double, 1 single, all with bath (one with Jacuzzi), phone, satellite TV, minibar, air conditioning
FACILITIES sitting rooms, dining room, breakfast room, garden, swimming pool
CREDIT CARDS AE, DC, MC, V
DISABLED not suitable **PETS** please check first
CLOSED mid-Jan to mid-Feb; restaurant only, Mon
LANGUAGES English
PROPRIETOR Valentino Petrangeli

TERNI

TITIGNANO

FATTORIA DI TITIGNANO
~ RURAL HAMLET GUESTHOUSE ~

Titignano, Orvieto, 05010 Terni
TEL (0763) 308022 **FAX** (0763) 308002

FATTTORIA DI TITIGNANO is not a place for people in search of refined luxury. It is a simple, honest, rural guesthouse whose attractions are not those of a professionally run, starred hotel but of a working farm estate that gives a warm welcome.

Owned by the aristocratic Corsini family and set in two thousand hectares, the hamlet stands on a hillside overlooking the Tiber Valley and Lake Corbara. On one side of the wide street (when we visited, it was being paved with cobble-stones at the expense of the European Community) is the principal house containing the public rooms and some of the bedrooms. A lovely *loggia* on the first floor, overlooks the church and the former farm workers' cottages, where there are more bedrooms and a few small apartments.

The general style is battered rustic with hints of former elegance: carved stone doors and fireplaces, gloomy oil paintings and high wooden ceilings. Bedrooms vary in size and decoration: in the farmers' cottages, they are smaller and more modern, and the excellent bathrooms have been newly installed. Make a point of visiting the wine cellars and the cheese dairy.

~

NEARBY Orvieto (25 km); Todi (23 km).
LOCATION 25 km NE of Orvieto, off the SS 79 bis
FOOD breakfast, dinner
PRICE € (30% discount for 3rd bed in room)
ROOMS 6 double, all with bath or shower; 5 apartments
FACILITIES sitting room, dining room, terrace, swimming pool
CREDIT CARDS not accepted
DISABLED not suitable **PETS** accepted
CLOSED never **LANGUAGES** English, French
MANAGERS Giulio and Monica Fontani

TERNI

LA CASELLA
RESTORED HAMLET

Ficulle, 05016 Terni

TEL & FAX (0763) 86684/86588
E-MAIL lacasella@tin.it
WEBSITE www.lacasella.com
FOOD breakfast, lunch, dinner
PRICE €-€€€
CLOSED never

L A CASELLA, A HAMLET of twelve houses built from local stone in the wooded hills north of Orvieto and isolated from the rest of the world by 7 km of unsurfaced road, is definitely for those in search of peace and quiet. The old houses, originally occupied by peasants and then abandoned, have been rescued and converted into cosy accommodation. The most romantic of the rooms have four-posters and open fires. The swimming pool, open from June to September, is in a field overlooking woods, and there is a riding centre and tennis courts, which are floodlit at night. A convivial atmosphere, communal dining, attractive bar plus a small health centre.

HOTEL NAMES

In this index, hotels are arranged in order of the first distinctive part of their names. Very common prefixes such as 'Hotel', 'Albergo', 'Il', 'La', 'Dei' and 'Delle' are omitted. More descriptive words such as 'Casa', 'Castello', 'Locanda' and 'Villa' are included.

Hotel Names

HOTEL NAMES

Hotel Locations

In this index, hotels are arranged in order of the names of the cities, towns or villages they are in or near. Hotels located in a very small village may be indexed under a larger place nearby. An index by hotel name precedes this one.

HOTEL LOCATIONS

Hotel Locations

SPECIAL OFFERS

Buy your *Charming Small Hotel Guide* by post directly from the publisher and you'll get a worthwhile discount. *

Titles available:	Retail price	Discount price
Austria	£10.99	£9.50
Britain & Ireland	£12.99	£11.50
Britain Bed & Breakfast	£10.99	£9.50
France	£13.99	£12.50
France Bed & Breakfast	£10.99	£9.50
Germany	£11.99	£10.50
Greece	£10.99	£9.50
Italy	£11.99	£10.50
Mallorca, Menorca & Ibiza	£9.99	£8.50
New England	£10.99	£9.50
Paris	£10.99	£9.50
Southern France	£10.99	£9.50
Spain	£11.99	£10.50
Switzerland	£9.99	£8.50
Venice and North-East Italy	£10.99	£9.50

Please send your order to:

Book Sales,

Duncan Petersen Publishing Ltd,

C7, Old Imperial Laundry, Warriner Gardens, London SW11 4XW

enclosing: 1) the title you require and number of copies

2) your name and address

3) your cheque made out to:

Duncan Petersen Publishing Ltd

*Offer applies to this edition and to UK only.

Visit charmingsmallhotels.co.uk
Our website has been completely rebuilt.
Please take a look - it includes fantastic
entries from all over Europe. It's the best
research tool on the web for our kind of
hotel.

Exchange rates
As we went to press, $1 bought 0.83 euros
and £1 bought 1.45 euros